FOUNDATIONAL CHRISTIANITY:

A Study of 1st John

By Bill Andrew

CROSSLINK
PUBLISHING

Foundational Christianity: A Study of 1ˢᵗ John

D CrossLink Publishing
C www.crosslink.org

Printed in the United States of America. All rights reserved under International Copyright law.

ISBN 978-1-936746-20-0

Table of Contents

Preface

T his work began as intensely personal and private. For a long time I had practiced a ritual of morning devotional reading and journaling as a way of cementing my relationship with God. Daily I read from several different devotional magazines or books, wrote down prayer requests and answers, and random thoughts.

One day commuting to my job, I read an issue of a magazine that in a 28 day span presented a summation of 1st John. It titled the study a "Primer On Christianity: Back To The Basics." Since I had, for some time, been trying to decide if I needed to go back to Bible teaching in a small group setting, this series intrigued me. I read it through, numerous times in fact. I became convinced I could take its framework and expand it into a fuller and more comprehensive survey of John's First Epistle.

I read the letter completely several times. I separated each reading by the study of different summary commentaries and outlines. Then I went back and highlighted in different colors the major themes as identified by other scholars. The final reading was detailed and time-consuming because I wrote down and read every cross-reference noted in my Bible.[1] I then dug into each of these verses and followed their cross-references until I was lead back to 1st John. All my findings I recorded in order in a spiral notebook. To "sanitize" my interpretations I did not read the Bible's study notes until *after* I had put my own down.

All this took about two years. At one point my wife Sandy and I were in a neighborhood Bible study and I was asked to "guest teach" one week. In our discussions I had mentioned my on-going project so the group asked me to share my work with them. At that time I had just barely completed my notes on Chapter One, so in about an hour I condensed my comments. I did not do a very good job and I wasn't too impressed with my work, either.

There was never an occasion during the course of the study for me to present the completed work, so I determined it was my assignment from God to write it all out in book form. And so this is what has come forth.

Throughout the time it took me to transform those spiral notebook entries, I got up each morning well before dawn and devoted what time I had before going to work to the project. I had no quota for each day's writing, only that I tried to deal as completely as I could with each verse as possible. Some verses, with corresponding "rabbit trails," took longer than others. Then I began to become more disciplined and sensible in my work. A few references I eliminated because they were either superfluous or my interpretation was badly out of alignment.

Sandy was patient and supportive. I shared, at a few points, some passages, and she was approving. She encouraged me to continue on with the project.

I took one short break during the time to create a short study of "WHICH MARY WAS AT THE TOMB?" to satisfy a personal curiosity as well as to answer a question that had arisen in a Bible study session.

After I completed a first version, I passed it along to a Christian brother, who is also a writer. Terry made some very practical suggestions that have been incorporated into this finished work. His guidance was helpful, but I give all the credit for inspiration to the Holy Spirit.

I am not a biblical scholar; I have had no scholastic theological training. A job with a denominational book publisher for nearly nine years taught me some basics of homiletics, exegesis, and hermeneutics. Sandy had given me a marvelous book years before on how to study the scriptures.[2] She'd also given me a fascinating New Testament version that explained Greek grammar and its impact on the deep meaning of passages.[3] I say all this to explain, *not to justify*, my interpretation. In some places I may be saying something totally at odds with the majority of Bible teachers and with archeological evidence. But it is *my* rendering, *my* supposition, what *I* understand the words to be saying *to me*. I invite you, I <u>challenge you</u>, to study this epistle for yourself. Do as I have done, pondering each verse, and find what message is there for <u>you</u>.

The Bible is a mystical, magical book. It is *alive*, breathing and morphing for every one who picks it up and opens it. It can bring to you the answers to your questions. Its solace can bring peace in the midst of tumult. You must do your part; but the joy you get from it is immeasurable.

Bill Andrew
November 5, 2012

Introduction

Bible study has one purpose: to encourage a personal relationship between individuals and the LORD God Almighty. That relationship comes from an understanding of Jesus Christ, His Son and our Savior and the work and personality of the Holy Spirit. From the beginning in Genesis through The Revelation, scripture's intention is to show God's plan of love and redemption; laid out before the reader is the design for reclaiming a life lost to sin through the satisfaction of Yahweh's demand for justice through blood sacrifice with the "once for all" sacrifice of Jesus Christ on the Cross. Each book, all 66 of them, has a point to make in that strategy. In some the central theme is less obvious than in others, but it is *always there*.

First John is to the study of the New Testament as Genesis is to the entire Bible. It introduces concepts essential for adherence to faith in Jesus as Savior. It is an overview of the basics of "New Testament faith." Initially one must grasp that moral standards and ethical behavior of the Old Testament were replaced by the Messiah's life and death and resurrection. The guide for living shifted; what was held as sufficient in the times of Moses, David, Jeremiah, and Isaiah no longer was applicable. Well, not really *not applicable*, but were adjusted to a new standard. The purpose of living changed from *personal survival* to *interpersonal relationships and a relationship with the Almighty and His Son*. After the resurrection, it became more important *how we lived with others* than the rules we followed *as we lived*.

Not that rules were unimportant; there were principles that had to be followed, a condition God makes clear never changes. Living absolutely free of values, doing as we pleased, most definitely is not in His design for eternal salvation. The granting of free-will to humans was God's way of saying, "*I want you to love and obey Me not because you have to but because you choose to*." God could have established a world in which our love was robotic, automatic, and not driven by anything other than a routine response.

But the LORD had a better idea. Even though we were given the capacity and ability to fall into sin, some inner sense made certain we wanted reconciliation. But restored fellowship was only achievable through God's intervention with a vehicle for grace and forgiveness. That vehicle was Jesus' life, death, and resurrection. Knowing this gift is offered without any prerequisite other than accepting Him as savior swells up within us such gratitude that affection for God is the only natural response. And that is how God desires it.

This is the essence of Christianity – our eternal destiny depends on our genuine passion for God's grace that is showered on us. This is an extension of the message of the Old Testament; it completes the search begun in Genesis by the Jewish nation for a connection between it and the Creator. That is another concept one has to grasp: the Old Testament and the New Testament are *not* two disparate volumes of Scripture. They dovetail by connecting the fruitless search by the Old Testament peoples with the solution of Christ. The failure of the Hebrews to remain faithful to Yahweh only furthered their dissatisfaction. That negative outlook would only be eradicated by the salvation offered by Jesus Christ.

But the greatest lesson of John's writings in the Gospel that bears his name, his three epistles, and his Revelation is that the only way to identify a true believer is by the manner and extent to which one exhibits *LOVE*. Comprehending that principle opens the heart and spirit to a full, personal, strong, and rewarding relationship with God, and with others. Establishing those relationships should be the goal of everyone.

Reading about and understanding the standard of Christian love *will not make you a loving person; making that change has to be a conscious and intentional lifestyle change.* But once you have started on that path, once you begin to enjoy the rewards of it, there will be no turning back. As you grow each day in your affection for God and others, and you perform more acts of service and solicitude, the greater will be the joy in your spirit.

And a happy spirit means a Christ-filled heart. It is a combination of feeling the joy of pure affection and acceptance for others resulting in the unconditional return from fellow believers that brings the cheerfulness into a Christian's life.

We have no definitive records on the personal lives of any of the Apostles, but evidence (by actions and word usage) seems to show that John was the youngest of the original twelve. The phrase "the disciple whom [Jesus] loved" is likely not a boast but a statement of fact. He was very sincerely attached to his Master. John's choice of words expresses that affection and clearly indicates it was more than the simple admiration of a student for a teacher; it was the emotional attachment of one who willingly submits his life to another, and places it squarely in their hands. This is the pure bond servant relationship of which the Apostle Paul writes so frequently. It is the trust John talks about so much in his epistles, the kind of trust we need to have for each other, and they have for us.

Church history and independent witness affirms John ministered in Jerusalem with much success, likely sharing with James (possibly the brother of Christ, who came to conversion after the resurrection) the leadership of the growing congregation there. These duties he performed in addition to caring for Mary, the mother of Jesus as per the instructions given him from the Cross by Our Lord. Because of his career-long close association with Peter there was not any competition or strife between them. John's brother James seems to have been an early martyr.

When the Romans destroyed Jerusalem, according to Christ's prediction, new directions needed to be taken. History relates that after the death of Christ's mother, John resided chiefly at Ephesus, quite possibly picking up the work Paul had started there, but in no way undermining or diminishing the work that apostle had done. Because of his influence and reputation (and the growing strength of the Christian movement) towards the close of Domitian's reign John was banished to the isle of Patmos, where he wrote his Revelation. On the accession of Nerva, he was set at liberty, and returned to Ephesus. There is evidence he wrote his Gospel around 85 A.D., a decade after Matthew who wrote somewhere between 50–75, Mark (65–70), and Luke (59–75). His Epistles were written around 90 A.D., likely in quick succession. His Revelation, sprouting from his experience on Patmos, could have been composed as early as 75 and as late as 95 A.D. Jude's composition closed the New Testament writings.

What about these other gospels and their writers? Matthew, like John, was an eye witness. He wrote for Jewish readers an account of Christ's ministry. His text is filled with allusions familiar to Hebrews, and the writing is slanted to appeal to the Hebraic tradition. Matthew confirms Christ as the fulfillment of Old Testament prophecy. Its points seal the argument of Jesus as Messiah.

Mark was not a total eyewitness, He was a friend of Paul, though he didn't seem to have the dedication to the mission field of that apostle. He may have been the young man who fled at Christ's arrest and ran away naked. His writing is flavored with the explanation of the suffering of Christ for our sins. Because he seems to have joined the band of disciples towards the end of Jesus' ministry, his gospel lacks many details of the others. It is certainly the breeziest of the four, being only 16 chapters. I have the personal conviction that his writing of the gospel was an attempt to make amends to Paul for his abandonment of the mission field.

Luke was not an eyewitness, nor a friend. He was a physician, trained in Greek healing, who was introduced to the faith and accepted it. He wanted his friend Theophilus to understand this new religion so he set about gathering details and information. He appears to have personally interviewed many, including (by tradition) Mary the mother of Jesus before she died (and presumably while she was still under the care of John). He then joined Paul and the work of the spreading of the church he recorded in The Acts of the Apostles, a second volume he sent to Theophilus.

John was another eye witness. His gospel tells the world who Christ truly was, His real nature, His actual authority, *and the personality of the* Divine Teacher. John wanted his readers to be certain they knew Christ came to instruct and to redeem mankind. That's why John used in his narrative those passages of our Savior's life which most clearly displayed His Divine power and authority; and those of His speeches in which He spoke most plainly of His own nature, and of the power of His death, as an atonement for the sins of the world. With John's gospel being the last of the four written, he had the luxury of being selective in which events he chose to report, using only those that strengthened his presentation of Christ as the actual, real, total embodiment of God. This strategy not only reinforces John's contentions, but gives validity to the events Matthew, Mark, and Luke set down by *not challenging them*. This is a significant point of biblical interpretation. Had there been any deceit in the other three Gospels, John most certainly would have exposed them. But he did not, so their accuracy must be presumed.

The slight variations in the gospel accounts need to be understood. No two people will report the same details of an event to which they are eyewitnesses. Some people concentrate on sounds, some on colors, some on movement, some on gestures. The glory of humanity is that each of us is individual and each can and does have his own will and nature. The Synoptic Gospels, as the other three are called, should be viewed as *complementary*, not *contradictory*. The failure of some of the world to accept the testimony of these four writers rests not on the writers but on the hearers. Because they write of supernatural things, and the world tries hard to discount the supernatural, it is not surprising the story of Jesus as told by Matthew, Mark, Luke, and John is challenged and denied. The irony is all were seeking to prove the supernatural did exist in Christ because He *was* supernatural, the Son of God.

The Gospel of John is written for us to *believe* in Christ; 1st John is written for us to *know what we believe.* It is written for believers, not for unbelievers. The warnings and lessons are for Christians, not for the unsaved world. This is an important point, one John will emphasize in the opening verses of his first letter: he was there, he knew what was happening. If there were something floating around in the traditions of the early church that were not based on fact, John would have been the first to issue the correction.

Our assumptions for John's writing of 1st John can be set aside when we read the epistle and see that he clearly states his reasons for writing when we read John 20:30-31:[4]

And truly Jesus did many other signs in the presence of His disciples, which are not written in this book;

but these are written that you may believe that Jesus is the Christ, the Son of God, and that believing you may have life in His name.

And in his first epistle, he says in Chapter 5, as a summation, what his purpose for writing the epistle was:

These things I have written to you who believe in the name of the Son of God, that you may know that you have eternal life, and that you may continue to believe in the name of the Son of God.

1ˢᵗ John 5:13

In the first chapter, he sets out before the readers what he intends to do.

That which was from the beginning, which we have heard, which we have seen with our eyes, which we have looked upon, and our hands have handled, concerning the Word of life-

the life was manifested, and we have seen, and bear witness, and declare to you that eternal life which was with the Father and was manifested to us-

that which we have seen and heard we declare to you, that you also may have fellowship with us; and truly our fellowship is with the Father and with His Son Jesus Christ.

And these things we write to you that your joy may be full.

1ˢᵗ John 1:1–4

There is speculation the gospel and the first epistle of John were circulated among the early believers together, since they have common themes, style, and intent. And, looking carefully at the structure and emphasis of 1st John, it could easily serve as a "commentary" on the gospel account. In the Gospel John recounts the miracles and teachings that absolutely identify Christ as divine. The evidence mounts up to support this in every chapter. In 1st John, the stress is on how *we* know we are Christians, and what being Christians is all about.

John, as a writer, is skilled in presenting arguments, then returning again and again to them with clarifying points and expansions of the central theses. Despite this, he is difficult to outline because there is no orderly flow; topics leapfrog back and forth, intertwining and buttressing each other. A careful, ordered presentation of arguments was a trademark of other early Christian epistles. Paul was a master of a "legalese" style; John's work seems to be less organized but definitely more personal. One gets the impression John was racing, struggling to get his thoughts down quickly; perhaps he was experiencing a sense of his own mortality. Tradition says John was the only one of the original apostles to have died a natural death. Maybe the growing threat to the faith by the Roman persecution weighed heavily on him, and he felt compelled to complete his exposition of the nature of faith in Christ. Any excuse we put forward is speculation; however keeping in mind that as his motivation will help us tolerate John's seemingly wild swings from one topic to another.

Who Was Jesus? – 1st John 1:1-3

L ook at the opening verses of the letter:

That which was from the beginning, which we have heard, which we have seen with our eyes, which we have looked upon, and our hands have handled, concerning the Word of life-

the life was manifested, and we have seen, and bear witness, and declare to you that eternal life which was with the Father and was manifested to us-

1ˢᵗ John 1:1-2

The "which" in the first verse is the same as in the opening verses of John's gospel.

In the beginning was the Word, and the Word was with God, and the Word was God.

John 1:1

That's right, *the Word* was "in" the beginning and John and the other disciples heard that Word, saw it with their own eyes, and touched it with their own hands. Naturally, that Word was Christ, but John is using the Greek word *logos.* "Logos" means a thought or concept; the expression or thought utterance. As a designation of Christ *logos* is peculiarly important because in Him are embodied all the treasures of divine wisdom, the collective "thought" of God and, He is "from" eternity. Jesus was in His incarnation the expression of the Person of God, and the "thought" of the Deity. *Logos* connotes that in the Being, Person, and work of Christ, God's nature is expressed fully.

The symbolism of "three," as in the Trinity, is continued through the three forms of logos: Jesus Christ is the living word. The Bible, all scripture, is the written word. The Holy Spirit, who communicates to us through our thoughts, is the spoken word.

John emphasizes throughout 1st John the reality of his experience and relationship with Christ. He wants his readers to know he, John, experienced logos personally. It is something he communicated from the very beginning of his writing in the gospel.

> *And the Word became flesh and dwelt among us, and we beheld His glory, the glory as of the only begotten of the Father, full of grace and truth.*

> *John 1:14*

Jesus physically existed; He could be seen, felt, touched, spoken to and heard from. This is critical; without the acknowledgment that Jesus was the living, breathing and actual personification of God, then there is no acceptance of His power to forgive sin and promise everlasting life. The disciples were taught by Christ, and He was real in every sense of the word. John was well aware that Peter, another of the disciples who was revered by believers had written

> *For we did not follow cunningly devised fables when we made known to you the power and coming of our Lord Jesus Christ, but were eyewitnesses of His majesty.*

> *For he received from God the Father honor and glory when such a voice came to Him from the Excellent Glory: "This is My beloved Son, in whom I am well pleased."*

> *And we heard this voice which came from heaven when we were with Him on the holy mountain.*

> *And so we have the prophetic word confirmed, which you do well to heed as a light that shines in a dark place, until the day dawns and the morning star rises in your hearts;*

> *2 Peter 1:16-19*

So these men are "eyewitnesses" to the Coming. They have credibility. They are respected. What they have to say is true. John early on establishes the authority of his writing. And their writings are as alive today as they were the days when styli scratched on scroll.

Luke quotes Christ as he points out evidence to the witnesses that authenticate His resurrection.

> *"Behold My hands and My feet, that it is I Myself. Handle Me and see, for a spirit does not have flesh and bones as you see I have."*
>
> *Luke 24:39*

The link is forged even stronger by comparing the Luke passage and 1ˢᵗ John 1:1 – "My hands" and "our hands." The reference is hardly subtle and certainly is consistent.

> *When he had said this, he showed them His hands and His side. Then the disciples were glad when they saw the Lord.*
>
> *John 20:20*

After the resurrection, Christ was physically present, and spoke with His friends. But, before His crucifixion, Jesus told them

> *Most assuredly, I say to you that you will weep and lament, but the world will rejoice; and you will be sorrowful, but your sorrow will be turned into joy.*
>
> *[...]*
>
> *Therefore you now have sorrow; but I will see you again and your heart will rejoice, and your joy no one will take from you.*
>
> *John 16:20,22*

So Jesus, to turn their grief into this joy, had to present to them His physical body. And it would have had to be a *physical* body, <u>not a ghostly or spiritual representation,</u> to satisfy their doubts and to meet Christ's own requirements of bringing them joy.

Thomas accepted the evidence before him:

3

> *Then he said to Thomas, "Reach your finger here, and look at My hands; and reach your hand here, and put it into My side. Do not be unbelieving, but believing."*
>
> *And Thomas answered and said to Him, "My Lord and my God!"*

John 20:27-28

How did Thomas and the others know Jesus was Messiah? Because the wounds He suffered, the wounds that were exhibited on His body had been written about hundreds of years before they were inflicted.

> *For dogs have surrounded Me; The congregation of the wicked has enclosed Me. They pierced My hands and My feet;*

Psalms 22:16

And Zechariah even prophesied that the wounds would be examined by believers:

> *And I will pour on the house of David and on the inhabitants of Jerusalem the Spirit of grace and supplication; then they will look on Me whom they pierced. Yes, they will mourn for Him as one mourns for his only son, and grieve for Him as one grieves for a firstborn.*

Zechariah 12:10

Jesus knew there would be some who didn't accept the testimony of those who witnessed His resurrected body.

> *Later he appeared to the eleven as they sat at the table; and he rebuked their unbelief and hardness of heart, because they did not believe those who had seen Him after he had risen.*

Mark 16:14

From this "rebuke" by the LORD it is very clear that acceptance of His bodily resurrection is a primary requirement of faith in Him.

Paul writes

> *For I delivered to you first of all that which I also received: that Christ died for our sins according to the Scriptures,*
>
> *and that he was buried, and that he rose again the third day according to the Scriptures,*
>
> *and that he was seen by Cephas, then by the twelve.*
>
> *After that he was seen by over five hundred brethren at once, of whom the greater part remain to the present, but some have fallen asleep.*
>
> *After that he was seen by James, then by all the apostles.*
>
> *Then last of all he was seen by me also, as by one born out of due time.*
>
> *1ˢᵗ Corinthian 15:3–8*

in order to again emphasize to new believers, and to refresh old believers, of the foundational truth that Christ lived as God/Man on earth, that He died for our sins, was buried, but rose again, bodily, as proof that our sins have been forgiven.

The "manifestation" of the mystery, cited in 1ˢᵗ John 1:2 is repeated by Paul in a doxology he records in Romans:

> *Now to Him who is able to establish you according to my gospel and the preaching of Jesus Christ, according to the revelation of the mystery kept secret since the world began*
>
> *but now has been made manifest, and by the prophetic Scriptures has been made known to all nations, according to the commandment of the everlasting God, for obedience to the faith*

to God, alone wise, be glory through Jesus Christ forever. Amen

Romans 16:25–27

The point is now clear; Jesus <u>had</u> to be physically evident as God in a human body, and unmistakably physically resurrected for His claims of forgiveness to be valid. This was supported and verified by the 12 apostles, and by the "over five hundred brethren;" the story had to be real. *It must be believed.*

To bring us full circle, back to the point of the authority on which this information is cited,

This is the disciple who gives witness about these things and who put them in writing: and we have knowledge that his witness is true.

John 21:25

The Light – 1st John 1:4-7

In 1:3, John says that a goal of his writing is for us to have "fellowship" with Him (and other believers); he is talking About "*koinonia,*" a Greek word meaning association, community, communion, joint participation, and intimacy. It is the concept of an individual being part of a greater group, but the group having just one purpose and goal. This is more than just a "getting together;" to the early believers this was a blending, bonding, and essential part of their faith-life. Acts 2:42 describes it: "And they continued steadfastly in the apostles' doctrine and fellowship, and in breaking of bread, and in prayers." This strong union, this elementary connection, is what John wants every believer to have with every other believer. From it, we will see, comes all the other attitudes of a Christian. It is the reward of a deep personal relationship with Jesus Christ.

When one experiences "*koinonia*" with others the bond is remarkable. Through the strength of each other, survival and victory become more attainable, and certainly more expectant. Faith is strengthened, and fears are pushed to the side. Individuals become powerful in the LORD beyond their own comprehension. Mighty works are accomplished for the good of God. And the "*koinonia,*" atmosphere becomes pervasive in each person and in the entire fellowship. John knew of that power, had witnessed it through the ending years of his life. He didn't want the believers, and especially the second generation of believers, to forget it. They had to hold on for the faith to grow and sustain itself, especially since great persecution was ahead. John had either already experienced The Revelation, or his personal spirit knew what was to come. Encouragement, faith, and a strong foundation – these the believers must have it to face what would come at them.

And these things write we unto you, that your joy may be full.

1st John 1:4

7

John continues his reasons for writing this epistle. He wishes that the readers will gain more than just knowledge, but that the knowledge will have an impact on their lives. Their lives need to be filled with the unsurpassed joy of having Christ as ruler of their existence. A fellowship so deep, so pervasive, it results in a comfort that ultimately is carefree; one is released from the agonies about salvation and eternity and the fears of daily living.

People complain that Christianity doesn't bring them freedom from tribulations; it only seems to bring on more. They are missing the point of "joy may be full." The fullness John and others speak of is in the satisfaction, the thrill of knowing your eternal destination is settled. A Christian, a believer, has no doubt of where they will end up when they die. Jesus has made a place for them in heaven, and that is where they are going. There may be travails daily as we walk, but when we sit down after our death, we're going to sit down at His feet and _rest_.

> *These things have I spoken unto you, that my joy might remain in you, and that your joy might be full.*
>
> *John 15:11*

Jesus tells His disciples plainly this was His intention in coming as a human. He knew the only way we could experience complete joy would be through salvation. Whatever it took, however it was to be done – even His sacrificial death on a cross – had to be done so we could experience joyfulness in spiritual communion with Him. Our writer John echoes this purpose as he tells us why he wrote this letter. The only way we can understand and appreciate this happiness is by comprehending what it means to be in unity with Christ.

But Jesus wanted believers to be clear on how this delight can be accomplished.

> *Hitherto have ye asked nothing in my name: ask, and ye shall receive, that your joy may be full.*
>
> *John 16:24*

Now, what does this "ask, and ye shall receive" mean? What is he talking about? What are we to ask for? Does He really mean it?

These things have I spoken unto you in proverbs: but the time cometh, when I shall no more speak unto you in proverbs, but I shall show you plainly of the Father.

At that day ye shall ask in my name: and I say not unto you, that I will pray the Father for you:

For the Father himself loveth you, because ye have loved me, and have believed that I came out from God.

I came forth from the Father, and am come into the world: again, I leave the world, and go to the Father.

John 16:25–28

This is a expansive way of saying that God's affection for us is so complete that He will grant anything we need for our joy simply because we accept Jesus as His Son and His power to forgive us of our sins. Because we believe the sacrifice of Christ on the cross erases our sinfulness, and because the LORD Himself accepts that sacrifice, our happiness is His intention for our lives.

"Ask" means to beg, call for, crave, desire, or require.

John sees this as vital, cornerstone, keystone, of how Christians should live. Failure to understand how expansive God's love is, how complete the sacrifice of His Son was means our wickedness is not absolved. Not comprehending the power we have as sons and daughters of the Most High means we are missing the comfort, reassurance, and strength we have been granted.

The People's New Testament Commentary[5] amplifies verse 24, which precedes this passage as the only way we can approach God is "through" Christ's name. We must accept and appropriate Jesus' power for us by making the request in the name of our Savior. Acknowledgment of that is a prerequisite for our petitions.

We've waded through John's explanation of why he is writing, a necessity to the study of any biblical book — purpose clarifies intent, if the two are not exactly the same thing. Now, in verse 5, John directly speaks what it is he wants to say.

> *This is the message which we have heard from Him and declare to you, that God is light and in Him is no darkness at all.*
>
> *1ˢᵗ John 1:5*

There it is, plainly laid out and spoken – "God is light and in Him is no darkness at all."

"Plainly?" you say? What does this mean? What does God's being light entail?

Christians believe light is a symbol of all that is lovely, beautiful, holy, good, desirable, righteous and lovable. This is the direct antithesis of the concept pagans had of a god; to them, the master of everything was full of hatred, vengeance and generated fear in those ignorant of him. Such a god was to be satisfied only with sacrifice and offerings. A pagan deity was not one to be loved or with which an association and relationship should be developed.

A practical aspect of John's use of "light" as a description of God differentiates the concept of the Almighty from the intellectual "enlightenment" of those who sought to dispel belief in the LORD. To link the goodness of God to light naturally put the antithesis, unrighteousness and disbelief, into "darkness." Those who adhered to these false teaching were "of darkness."

Note carefully John says there is no darkness "in Him," that is, there is no darkness in the nature of God. It is quite possible, and indeed likely, based on the track record of mankind, for it to be dark in His presence. Were there not darkness in the world, there would be no need for the Savior.

Now, how can we be certain that this statement – this declaration that God is light and there is no darkness in Him – is true? Look at the source of the information: "*ye have heard it from Him.*" Christ has heard it from God (not difficult since God is Christ and Christ is God), but the significance is it is coming from *the* ultimate source. What was told to the disciples is being repeated to us by John.

> *All things have been delivered to Me by My Father, and no one knows the Son except the Father. Nor does*

anyone know the Father except the Son, and the one to whom the Son wills to reveal Him.

Matthew 11:27

Christ Himself confirms anything He says is a direct "quote" from God. After all, Jesus is the incarnation of God. The concept gets confusing but at the same time it is astounding. God speaks through Jesus Christ; Jesus Christ speaks to us with His words; the Holy Spirit communicates to us what God wants us to know by revealing a message to us in our hearts and our conscience. Believers have direct communication as well as communion with God.

And Jesus came and spoke to them, saying, "All authority has been given to Me in heaven and on earth.

Matthew 28:18

Jesus verifies to the disciples His sanction to speak these truths. This establishes His authority. Those who believe in Him can be assured that what He says is exactly what God says.

No one has seen God at any time. The only begotten Son, who is in the bosom of the Father, he has declared Him.

John 1:18

Not that anyone has seen the Father, except he who is from God; he has seen the Father.

John 6:46

As the Father knows Me, even so I know the Father; and I lay down My life for the sheep.

John 10:15

John in his gospel and here again in 1ˢᵗ John affirms the right of Jesus to speak for the heavenly father. This means in reading 1ˢᵗ John what is said is true; not earthly truth, but heavenly truth, eternal truth. There can be no argument or disputation of it. Keep this in mind as John in later verses assaults what others are asserting to be "truth."

> *If we say that we have fellowship with Him, and walk in darkness, we lie and do not practice the truth.*

> *1ˢᵗ John 1:6*

John carefully begins his thesis. If we claim fellowship, claim to be believers in Christ but our lives show that we are not, then we are living a lie. We've just seen the nature of God is "light;" physics tells us the absence of light is "darkness." The two are mutually exclusive and cannot co-exist. One must either be "of light" or "of darkness."

> *he reveals deep and secret things; he knows what is in the darkness, And light dwells with Him.*

> *Daniel 2:22*

From Old Testament times, the LORD has been viewed as "light," so John's presentation of this concept is not groundbreaking. From looking at this passage in Daniel, even the idea of a coexistent "light" is not foreign.

> *For with You is the fountain of life; In Your light we see light.*

> *Psalms 36:9*

Whatever "light" is, we recognize it in God.

> *There is a man in your kingdom in whom is the Spirit of the Holy God. And in the days of your father, light and understanding and wisdom, like the wisdom of the gods, were found in him; and King Nebuchadnezzar your father-your father the king-made him chief of the magicians, astrologers, Chaldeans, and soothsayers.*

> *Daniel 5:11*

In this passage Daniel defines the "light" that is in the LORD to be knowledge and understanding and wisdom.

Every good gift and every perfect gift is from above, and comes down from the Father of lights, with whom there is no variation or shadow of turning.

James 1:17

And here is the New Testament parallel – James identifying God as the Father of "lights," the source of every good thing. This alone makes God so much more than mankind can imagine.

God is not a man, that he should lie, Nor a son of man, that he should repent. Has he said, and will he not do? Or has he spoken, and will he not make it good?

Numbers 23:19

Moses makes it clear that God is not like man; His differences are so great we cannot full comprehend His character; *faith* is necessary to deal with this fact. The concept is too massive for us to fully understand, but we must do so for our lives to be devoted to Him.

And we return to John's Gospel for the capstone of the concept of Jesus' authority to tell us of God and the certainty that what He says is true:

Not that anyone has seen the Father, except he who is from God; he has seen the Father.

John 6:46

Grasping the concept that "light" represents goodness, and all that encompasses, is necessary to clearly understand what John means when he speaks about the opposite of "light," "darkness."

Because of The Fall, man's natural condition is evil, blackness, darkness; there is an absolute lack of divine truth in the sinful, natural man. Christ came to replace that with His light, the light of truth. The conflict, the eternal and everlasting struggle, is that darkness and light cannot co-exist. One must be supplanted and replaced by the other. The one chosen by each individual is the choice between believers and non-believers.

"Living in darkness" is more than having a sinful nature. Darkness, being the absence of light, means motives, goals, concepts, justifications, rationalizations – *everything* – is steeped in evil. Nothing good can come of it. There is no intention to live a righteous life. Acknowledgment of this sad fact has to be the turning point in one's life.

When one faces the choice of living a life that is black or a living a life of glory, there hardly seems to be a choice.

> *"I have come as a light into the world, that whoever believes in Me should not abide in darkness."*

> *John 12:46*

Jesus is the answer, the solution. Here, in plain words He says all we have to do to avoid living in the darkness is to believe in Him. Further examination of the "light" offered by Christ assures us of happiness, and fulfillment; darkness does not. Anything earthly or human that is at enmity with God is darkness. A life of darkness is emblematic of sin, morally and spiritually depraved. "Light" is the intellectual, moral, and ethical standard by which our lives are measured.

All this is understood by John's readers; he doesn't have to spell it out in the epistle because it has been part of his teaching from the beginning; Christians learned all this when they came into the family of believers. But the *comprehension* of it **is essential** to the understanding and appreciation of what John is saying. There must be full agreement and acceptance of his postulates to recognize the value of what the apostle writes.

Now John begins to explain how this principle works in every day living. One cannot proclaim to be a believer, a follower of Christ *(a claim)* and live sinfully *(an exhibition)*. **The proclamation of a life(style) is louder than our proclamation of faith.**

John cites an example of this contradiction.

> *he who says he is in the light, and hates his brother, is in darkness until now.*

> *he who loves his brother abides in the light, and there is no cause for stumbling in him.*

> *But he who hates his brother is in darkness and walks*
> *in darkness, and does not know where he is going,*
> *because the darkness has blinded his eyes.*
>
> *1ˢᵗ John 2:9–11*

Our true relationship with the Father is revealed in the way we relate to our earthly companions. It is that simple. We can't be one way with people and another way with the LORD; our spiritual nature won't permit it. And that nature is the very thing John wants us to get under control.

The challenge for the Christian is to live *in* this world but not to live *as* the world. If we submit ourselves and everything we do to the guidance of the Holy Spirit (and that happens *only* when our faith is genuine) then it is possible to resist the call of the world. This doesn't mean that we won't feel the tug of worldliness; Jesus did not promise us all pleasantness and ease if we followed Him; in fact, the more we strive to live a Christ-like life, the harder Satan will pursue us. The battle is fiercer for the believer because to *destroy* one is a greater victory for the Devil than *claiming* one *already fallen*.

> *But if we walk in the light as he is in the light, we have*
> *fellowship with one another, and the blood of Jesus*
> *Christ His Son cleanses us from all sin.*
>
> *1ˢᵗ John 1:7*

John will repeat this "proof" over and over. If we are followers of Jesus living with His example as our guide, then we are living in association, community, communion, joint participation, and intimacy with other believers. Our behavior will identify us as His followers. That behavior *will not lie*; it will tell the world who and what we are. In God's economy, there are not "two sides" to a coin. What is on one side will be on the other. It is an absolute truth, and one which cannot be avoided. Character, or at least what is represented as character, in God's view is totally transparent.

O house of Jacob, come and let us walk In the light of the Lord.

Isaiah 2:5

The prophet's call is for the people of Israel (and us, the children of God) to follow in the example of the LORD. Doing so exhibits our trust in God's promise to ultimately resolve all our conflicts. We are to let His light "illuminate" our path; it is a call to reverse the way we have been living (repentance) with the result our lives will fulfill His purpose for us.

For you were once darkness, but now you are light in the Lord. Walk as children of light.

Ephesians 5:8

This is the Apostle Paul's New Testament echo of Isaiah's cry. It is the same context, the same command and the same result. Paul anticipates our having come out of the darkness.

You are all sons of light and sons of the day. We are not of the night nor of darkness.

1ˢᵗ Thessalonians 5:5

This concept of "light" and "darkness" is so essential, we need to read Christ's explanation of the impact of it on our living once more.

"No one, when he has lit a lamp, puts it in a secret place or under a basket, but on a lamp stand, that those who come in may see the light.

"The lamp of the body is the eye. Therefore, when your eye is good, your whole body also is full of light. But when your eye is bad, your body also is full of darkness.

"Therefore take heed that the light which is in you is not darkness.

"If then your whole body is full of light, having no part dark, the whole body will be full of light, as when the bright shining of a lamp gives you light."

Luke 11:33-36

"Darkness" is a metaphor for an evil spiritual, moral, ethical, intellectual behavior and life style. Anything that is not reflective of the goodness of God and His creation is "dark." But Jesus makes a new point. The source of this darkness is not always our natural-born sinfulness. It came spring from ignorance, willful disobedience, willful and intentional blindness. Each of these conditions could be corrected of our own volition, so remaining in those states is our responsibility. We cannot escape judgment or excuse it in our lives by claiming "I'm just made that way." The blackness Christ condemns (and that John is teaching about) is purposeful and premeditated. One chooses that life style deliberately, but by God's grace, we can elect to change it.

One might argue our sinfulness is a natural consequence of the Fall of Man. But, as we will see later when we come across passages from Romans, God has implanted in each and every creation a small seed of knowledge of Him, and the desire to know more of it. We have the elective choice to follow a path different; the way of evil is not pre-determined for us. We can choose to lift ourselves out of it.

Verse 1:7 sets clearly the prerequisites and the outcome of living in the "darkness." What is the solution, how can one, apart from making the conscious shift in lifestyle, avoid the judgment?

the blood of Jesus Christ His Son cleanses us from all sin.

1ˢᵗ John 1:7

Now we are moving into the "good news," the "gospel" John wants to be certain we understand. "The blood" is the atoning, sacrificial death of Jesus Christ on the cross as payment for our sins. It is the one-time act to satisfy God's requirement for punishment for sinfulness. But the *power* of Jesus' death is an ongoing, perpetual act of cleansing, forgiveness, and redemption. Our *acknowledgment* of that act and *claiming* the absolution is what "saves" us and makes us

Christians. The mechanics of accepting Jesus as savior are very simple.

You admit you are sinful and in need of redemption, that without it you are living in a world of darkness and will face judgment for that lifestyle;

You agree that some sacrifice or counterbalance for your wickedness is required to assure your acceptability to God;

You agree Christ's death on the cross is the means of offsetting that sinfulness.

That, in its simplest form, is the essence of accepting Christ as your savior.

Verses 6 and 7 are the first of three pairs of verses in Chapter 1 in which John presents "tests" of faith. In each instance he will describe a condition and then offer the solution. These tests are his way of giving believers a checklist of their own situation. The beauty of the writing's structure is he just doesn't trot out the problem, but provides a resolution – .the grace of Christ's sacrificial death for our sinful nature.

Having been cleansed by Jesus' blood sacrifice, we become examples of the Light. We are outward and obvious signs of that which dwells within us. Loving one another is the first and most apparent mark.

Having No Sin – 1st John 1:8-10

T he next verse presents a seeming contradiction for us.

If we say that we have no sin, we deceive ourselves, and the truth is not in us.

1ˢᵗ John 1:8

How do we "have no sin" but deceive ourselves and don't have the truth in us? We just learned that our sins have been forgiven by Christ. What's going on here?

In this case, John is speaking of constant, continual, repetitious sin. The "sin" in this context is an aggregate sinfulness, a collection of many instances. (It can refer to a group of persons' communal sin or sins, or an individual's repetition of sinful acts.) Those being the case, occasional or unintentional sins are not held against us. And, because of our relationship with Christ, when we do slip-up, our spirit is so grieved and affected we seek forgiveness through confession and repentance; we do not remain in a sinful condition. John speaks here of the person who is not moved by their behavior to seek forgiveness., but tries to portray to the world that they do not live that kind of life. Denial of the truth of it is only confirmation of the darkness of that kind of life; the circle spirals in on itself.

"The truth" – that which is *not* in such a person, is clarity, reality, accuracy, integrity, dependability, and propriety. The reflection to the world is not just in the correctness of our declarations, but of our character. It is the deficiency in our personality that faith in Christ will overcome. It is the shortcoming most easily remedied, but the one most resisted.

Why do people lie? Telling the truth is so easy, so simple. But fabrications are used to cover up missteps and failings in our lives. Lies are told to satisfy a crushed or defeated ego. They are used to make one "feel" better about themselves. They are used to cover mistakes that are made. People tell lies to impress others, to represent falsely their significance and importance. In short, lies are a means of making others think differently about us instead of having them feel about us as we are.

Lying is also a way of covering our own feelings of inadequacy and – pardon the phrase, for it has become so overworked – "low self-esteem." By modifying the truth we can make ourselves out to be much better than we ***think*** we are.

> *If we confess our sins, [then] he is faithful and just to forgive us our sins and to cleanse us from all unrighteousness.*
>
> *1ˢᵗ John 1:9*

This is the second of the "If … then" statements John presents. Again, it is a situation followed by the solution. The "if" portion is always a condition of our humanness, a representation of what we are; "then" is always our way of curing and replacing that negative with His positive.

Instead of affirming we are sinless we should confess our sins. If we confess our sins the Lord will keep his promise of mercy, and be just in applying the atonement of Christian forgiveness of our sins. This is the remedy to this problem of lying, and especially about our lying about our aberrant behavior.

There are more consequences to disavowing our sinfulness than the threat to our eternal soul; though that is major.

> *When I kept silent, my bones grew old Through my groaning all the day long.*
>
> *Psalms 32:3*

> *There is no soundness in my flesh Because of Your anger, Nor any health in my bones Because of my sin.*
>
> *Psalms 38:3*

Medical science has shown there are physical and physiological costs to emotional stress. The incredible strain of living a double life – one in which we deny we are doing wrong, and one in which we are not living a righteous life – puts an enormous burden on us. The mental exertion of attempting to keep stories straight, as lies are piled on top of lies, is enormous. Many psychosomatic illnesses can be traced back to mental anguish over guilt. Keeping short accounts with the LORD, seeking His forgiveness by confessing our sins is the best way to keep in good health.

> *being justified freely by His grace through the redemption that is in Christ Jesus,*
>
> *whom God set forth as a propitiation by His blood, through faith, to demonstrate His righteousness, because in His forbearance God had passed over the sins that were previously committed,*
>
> *to demonstrate at the present time His righteousness, that he might be just and the justifies of the one who has faith in Jesus.*

> ***Romans 3:24–26***

Paul, in his classic Romans letter, explains the reasoning behind this forgiveness by God. The argument rests on the premise God must provide a way for us to balance our sinfulness and be returned to fellowship with Him.

"Propitiation" relates to an appeasing or expiating, having placating or expiating force; a means of appeasing. It describes the cover of the Ark of the Covenant in the Holy of Holies, which was sprinkled with the blood of the sacrificial animal on the annual Day of Atonement (This rite offered to God to the blood of the sacrifice, and signified the lives of the people, the loss of which they deserved because of their sins, were spared and by this ceremony God was appeased and their sins expiated); hence the "lid" of expiation. Its relationship to Christ is more as an expiatory sacrifice and an expiatory victim

With Christ's crucifixion, our unrighteousness is "set aside," replaced by the gift of Himself. His blood, shed on our behalf, satisfies the requirement for penalty.

> *Wash me thoroughly from my iniquity, And cleanse me from my sin.*

> ***Psalm 51:2***

The cleansing at the Cross is complete, total, once for all. There is no having to go back and do it again. The Day of Atonement ceremony had to be repeated every year. Through Jesus the sin debt is completely satisfied.

> *"I will cleanse them from all their iniquity by which they have sinned against Me, and I will pardon all their iniquities by which they have sinned and by which they have transgressed against Me.*

> *Jeremiah 33:8*

God wants it plainly understood what He forgives "all their iniquity by which they have sinned against Me." Not only certain failures, not only those within a specified time frame, but *everything*. Once we accept the sacrifice of Christ, then *every single sin we have committed, or will ever commit, is forgiven.* We cannot lose our salvation; it is sealed.

> *"Remember these, O Jacob, And Israel, for you are My servant; I have formed you, you are My servant; O Israel, you will not be forgotten by Me!*

> *I have blotted out, like a thick cloud, your transgressions, And like a cloud, your sins. Return to Me, for I have redeemed you."*

> *Sing, O heavens, for the Lord has done it! Shout, you lower parts of the earth; Break forth into singing, you mountains, O forest, and every tree in it! For the Lord has redeemed Jacob, And glorified Himself in Israel.*

> *Thus says the Lord, your Redeemer, And he who formed you from the womb: "I am the Lord, who makes all things, Who stretches out the heavens all alone, Who spreads abroad the earth by Myself;*

> *Isaiah 44:21–23*

Another Old Testament prophet, Jeremiah, agrees.

> *In those days and in that time," says the Lord, "The iniquity of Israel shall be sought, but there shall be*

> *none; And the sins of Judah, but they shall not be found; For I will pardon those whom I preserve.*
>
> **Jeremiah 50:20**

Isaiah hammers home the point:

> *"I, even I, am he who blots out your transgressions for My own sake; And I will not remember your sins.*
>
> **Isaiah 43:25**

> *I have blotted out, like a thick cloud, your transgressions, And like a cloud, your sins. Return to Me, for I have redeemed you."*
>
> **Isaiah 44:22**

One more passage in the Old Testament repeats the theme:

> *he will again have compassion on us, And will subdue our iniquities. You will cast all our sins Into the depths of the sea.*
>
> **Micah 7:19**

And finally, the writer of Hebrews brings it all down to the believer's perspective, of the totality and efficiency of the cleansing offered by God Almighty:

> *But Christ came as High Priest of the good things to come, with the greater and more perfect tabernacle not made with hands, that is, not of this creation.*
>
> *Not with the blood of goats and calves, but with His own blood he entered the Most Holy Place once for all, having obtained eternal redemption.*
>
> *For if the blood of bulls and goats and the ashes of a heifer, sprinkling the unclean, sanctifies for the purifying of the flesh,*
>
> *how much more shall the blood of Christ, who through the eternal Spirit offered Himself without spot to God,*

> *cleanse your conscience from dead works to serve the living God?*

> *Hebrews 9:11–14*

And now we come to the third and final "if ... then" completes in this first chapter of the letter.

> *If we say that we have not sinned, we make Him a liar, and His word is not in us.*

> *1ˢᵗ John 1:10*

If we say we have not sinned *then* we are lying because God says we *have* sinned. He declares "There is none righteous; no, not one" (Rom 3:10,Ps 14:4). Hence, if we assert that we are sinless we make God a liar. Our basic knowledge of human nature tells us this statement, "we have not sinned," cannot be true. Not only are we lying to others, but we are trying to lie to ourselves. And we are calling God a liar for having thus charged us as sinners.

Note the words concerning sin, found in verses 8-10 are <u>not</u> addressed to Gentile sinners, but the generation that had grown up in the church. Indeed, of all the epistles, this is the only one that can truly be said to have been addressed to a fully Christian generation. Hence, it would naturally emphasize, not the unconverted sinner's need of pardon, but the Christian's constant need of a pardoning Savior. Even though our salvation was sealed once and for all time with Christ's death, the true struggle of our lives is to remember that and live a life that is constantly moving towards a "Christ-like-ness." This perspective is essential to grasping the impact of the truths John sets out in his letter. It also reinforces his reference to his readers as "children" a term of deep affection and closeness; he would not feel that affinity to non-believers. John's desperation to convey this message is a reflection of his genuine affection for believers.

Chapter 1 comes to a close with this ringing challenge to those who scoff at the need for a savior, or who seek to represent themselves as superior. John has introduced "light" as a metaphor for God and His goodness, a principle every hearer could understand. John reveals his fondness and affection for his fellow believers with his deep concern that they grasp the consequences of mindless blanket assertions about sinfulness. He has introduced

But the beloved apostle is only getting started.

The Advocate – 1st John 2:1-2

C hapter and verse breaks in the Bible are artificial. Original manuscripts were written without any such indications. Writing materials were precious, so rarely was spacing substituted as a means of signifying a change in thought. Because of the grammatical structure of both Hebrew and Greek, many articles, antecedents, and pronouns that make texts clear to us today are not in the originals. Modern translations now put the scripture into paragraphs, sublimating verse markers. Some versions group thoughts together, and put the collective verse designations at the beginning of the passage.

This means when John was composing 1st John, he wasn't thinking of divisions in his writing. Because he seems to repeat a point of emphasis it is as though he had put the work aside, then picked it up again, and plunged ahead, not reviewing what he already had written. It is also likely John went back over certain themes because he was compelled as to their urgency and significance rather than inattention.

One must also remember few in the early church world could read; epistles from John, Paul, Peter, and the gospels were usually read aloud at meetings. The writers, knowing this, sometimes prepared their thoughts in "packages" that would be easily absorbed. Today's modern advertising is geared to the 15 second sound bite. With an average rate of 120 words per minute, that makes for a 30-word parcel to be comprehended. It is not unusual, then, for certain passages to be pithy, and for prime concepts to be repeated frequently. One can evaluate the significance a writer places on points by how often they are rephrased, reiterated and recurring.

The central theme of Chapter 2 is the righteous life. Chapter 1 focused on the incarnation of Christ and its power; now John begins his practical application by revealing the impact of that incarnation.

Because John wants us to grasp the veracity of his teaching, he tells us once more why he has written this letter.

> *My little children, these things I write to you, so that*
> *you may not sin. And if anyone sins, we have an*
> *Advocate with the Father, Jesus Christ the righteous.*
>
> *1ˢᵗ John 2:1*

But this time he is a bit more specific. In Chapter 1, when he states his purpose for the letter, he speaks in general terms. His justifications are broad, but strongly supportive of the authority by which he writes. In that portion of Chapter 1, it is as though he were presenting his credentials to reassure readers that what he has to say is true.

Here he is getting down to the practical specifics of living a Christian life. Remember, though, John is writing to believers; at this point he is not concerned with the unsaved. He says he doesn't want us to sin, so he's explaining to us Christ's power to assist us. John continues his "if …then" structure, telling us *if* we transgress *then* Jesus is available to us as a defender for us with God, the judge.

Paul was fond of using legal terms as he described the guilt upon us as humans. The use of legalese was, while not routine in conversations in biblical times, was customary enough that John uses it to describe our "advocate." An advocate was one who comes along side of us to take our side, to plead our case before an authority

> *Therefore he is also able to save to the uttermost those*
> *who come to God through Him, since he always lives to*
> *make intercession for them.*
>
> *For such a High Priest was fitting for us, who is holy,*
> *harmless, undefiled, separate from sinners, and has*
> *become higher than the heavens;*
>
> *who does not need daily, as those high priests, to offer*
> *up sacrifices, first for His own sins and then for the*
> *people's, for this he did once for all when he offered up*
> *Himself.*
>
> *Hebrews 7:25–27*

27

Such is how the writer of Hebrews further classifies Christ and His work for us. That author emphasizes, unlike the human priests of the old sacrificial system, Christ has performed all necessary for the forgiveness of sin. He died for it all. Now, having paid that price, He can stand before God and argue our case.

> *For Christ has not entered the holy places made with hands, which are copies of the true, but into heaven itself, now to appear in the presence of God for us;*
>
> *not that he should offer Himself often, as the high priest enters the Most Holy Place every year with blood of another-*
>
> *not that he should offer Himself often, as the high priest enters the Most Holy Place every year with blood of another*
>
> *And as it is appointed for men to die once, but after this the judgment,*
>
> *so Christ was offered once to bear the sins of many. To those who eagerly wait for Him he will appear a second time, apart from sin, for salvation.*

Hebrews 9:24–28

And the Hebrews' writer describes the process completely. Again, it must be understood John (*and* the writer of Hebrews) speaks to *believers*; it is only those for whom Christ died that He can and will intercede. His blood atonement is meaningless to those who do not believe in it.

We have an Advocate with the Father, One who carries on our cause for us on high. This is not in order to obtain righteousness, nor to wash our sins away. We are talking about the "divine righteousness" that has been placed us *into* the light, even as God Himself is in the light. But communion is interrupted. When communion is interrupted, when we have sinned, Christ intervenes for us.

Divine righteousness abides. The immutable foundation of our relationships with God is established on the blood of Christ. When communion, which exists only in the light, is interrupted, the intercession of Christ, available by virtue of His blood (for propitiation for the sin has also been made), restores the soul that it may again enjoy communion with God according to the light, into which righteousness has introduced it.

This is the "then" action of John's "If ... then" in 2:1. It is a structure John enjoys and utilizes numerous times in his epistles. Its logical form targets specific questions and presents the precise responses, giving the believer almost a check-list of rejoinders for situations. Readers today find them helpful guideposts to John's topics.

> *Now to Him who is able to keep you from stumbling,*
> *And to present you faultless Before the presence of His*
> *glory with exceeding joy,*

> *Jude 24*

Simply contemplating this magnificent concept, Jude breaks forth in admiration. In this doxology that is the benediction to his letter, Jude praises God for His ability to keep us from "stumbling." Believers must cling to the faith that the cleansing will be done and that we will be brought blameless into the presence of God. The conviction in one's heart that this is true seals the faith. Without it, then the concept is meaningless and life is hopeless.

To the human mind, it seems impossible for this to be done. But Paul says

> *Now to Him who is able to do exceedingly abundantly*
> *above all that we ask or think, according to the power*
> *that works in us,*

> *Ephesians 3:20*

This praise not only is of His ability to produce glorious results in our lives, but to do the seemingly unachievable of removing from our lives all sin and blackness. We can walk in the light because the Light has come into us when we acknowledge the Light's power to drive out the darkness. The argument may sound circular, and it is. But the sealing point in the circle is our acceptance of the forgiveness. That is the "deal maker."

How much is the "abundance" of which Paul speaks? The definition of "abundantly"[6] is "exceeding some number or measure or rank or need; over and above, more than is necessary, super-added; exceeding abundantly, supremely; something further, more, much more than all, more plainly; superior, extraordinary, surpassing, uncommon; preeminence, superiority, advantage, more eminent, more remarkable, more excellent." That's a pretty good bit. It is certainly more than we expect, and definitely more than we deserve. Yet this is the level to which God goes to grant to us favor and cleansing. The key to it coming about, though, is the acknowledgment of the gift. Until the reward is received, the offer of salvation is meaningless.

Paul tells us more about this advocacy mentioned in 1st John 2:1.

> *...It is Christ who died, and furthermore is also risen, who is even at the right hand of God, who also makes intercession for us.*
>
> **Romans 8:34**

> *For there is one God and one Mediator between God and men, the Man Christ Jesus,*
>
> **1st Timothy 2:5**

A "mediator" is one who intervenes between two (or more), either in order to make or restore peace and friendship, or for ratifying a covenant. Christ's role is active. He is also impartial (discounting His uniqueness as being Father and Son simultaneously) in that what He seeks is healing between a human soul and God. He seeks restoration of the fellowship that has been broken,.

> *And you, who once were alienated and enemies in your mind by wicked works, yet now he has reconciled*
>
> *in the body of His flesh through death, to present you holy, and blameless, and above reproach in His sight*
>
> **Colossians 1:22**

Through His body sacrifice, we are reconciled. There it is again, the completely voluntary but total surrender of His life for ours.

We return to John's description of this process. He says Christ is the "propitiation" for our sins.

> *And he Himself is the propitiation for our sins, and not*
> *for ours only but also for the whole world.*
>
> *1st John 2:2*

A "propitiation" is an intervention between two, either in order to make or restore peace and friendship, or to form a compact. Strong[7] extends the definition to include one who arbitrates, and who serves as a communicator. Jesus is serving several functions while He intercedes for us — He's defending us, He's calling forth mercy for us, He's accepting the punishment that should be ours. Any one of these tasks would be an immeasurable recompense for our sinfulness. Yet He is doing all of them, with our faith and belief His only reimbursement. And His propitiation is for *all* the sins of *all* the world.

This verse is the continuation of the "then" portion of the "if ... then" statement with which John opens the chapter. Remember, to John there was no break; this flows from his pen as a continuous thought. His reference to "My little children" clearly tells us he is writing to believers. The solution offered by Christ's sacrifice is only available to those who have the faith.

> *...whom God set forth as a propitiation by His blood,*
> *through faith, to demonstrate His righteousness,*
> *because in His forbearance God had passed over the*
> *sins that were previously committed,*
>
> *Romans 3:25*

Look at the Old Testament corollary:

> *"Then he* [the high priest] *shall kill the goat of the sin*
> *offering, which is for the people, bring its blood inside*
> *the veil, do with that blood as he did with the blood of*
> *the bull, and sprinkle it on the mercy seat and before*
> *the mercy seat.*

31

> *"So he shall make atonement for the Holy Place,*
> *because of the uncleanness of the children of Israel,*
> *and because of their transgressions, for all their sins;*
> *and so he shall do for the tabernacle of meeting which*
> *remains among them in the midst of their uncleanness."*
> [Moses, quoting the LORD]

> ***Leviticus 16:15–16***

Look at that carefully. It took the blood of two animals – a bull and a goat, two very valuable creatures in that economy – to make an *annual* atonement for the sins of just the Hebrews. Can you imagine how much more would have been required under the sacrificial system to provide for forgiveness for the *whole world <u>forever?</u>* I don't think Moses could have conceived such.

The Christ sacrifice is a bridge, closing the gap between humanity and God. But the faith **<u>and</u>** acceptance of the bridge must be by the sinner, not by God. God's character has not changed. Christ as a propitiation is a gift. The LORD'S attitude toward the sinner is deflected only because the sinner, now covered by the blood of Jesus, "looks" different to God. God can't see the stain of transgression. He sees only the regenerated believer. The sinfulness is invisible to the Almighty.

The wonder of it continues, in consideration of the "whole world" being cleansed.

> *The next day John[the Baptist] saw Jesus coming*
> *toward him, and said, "Behold! The Lamb of God who*
> *takes away the sin of the world!*

> ***John 1:29***

The Baptist proclaims to all within hearing what and who Jesus is. The "world" means the ungodly multitude, the whole mass of men alienated from God, and therefore hostile to the cause of Christ. And, at that point in history, that was everybody.

For I delivered to you first of all that which I also received: that Christ died for our sins according to the Scriptures,

1st Corinthians 15:3

This was the part of the gospel Paul took to the Gentiles, including the Corinthians. The other, the more important part of the good news, was the resurrection. Paul's point here, though, is the Old Testament – *the Scriptures* – wrote of this from the very beginning.

Christ, and only Christ, and *especially* Christ, has satisfied the sacrificial need for our forgiveness by *being* the sacrificial substitution. He traded His life for ours. It is glorious enough that He made the trade for us. Consider the magnanimity that the trade is for everyone in the future as well!

Abiding and Keeping – 1st John 2:3-6

Now by this we know that we know Him, if we keep His commandments.

1ˢᵗ John 2:3

T hat is the New King James version. In other translations it reads:

This is how we know that we know him: if we keep his commandments.

World English

And by this we may be certain that we have knowledge of him, if we keep his laws.

Basic English

here's how we can be sure that we know God in the right way: Keep [H]is commandments.

The Message

When we obey God, we are sure that we know [H]im.

The Contemporary English Version

And this is how we may discern [daily, by experience] that we are coming to know Him [to perceive, recognize, understand, and become better acquainted with Him]if we keep [bear in mind, observe, practice] His teachings [precepts, commandments].

The Amplified Bible

John's syntax is a little difficult to follow, and none of the translations seem to say it as plain as it should be said: "*If we keep the [laws, commandments] then we are certain we know Christ is our salvation.*"

"*Knowing*" is recognizing Jesus for whom and what He is. Following His commandments (the most notable of which is "Love one another")[8] reassure us we are part of the Kingdom. **Obedience is the key to reassurance.** Jesus' teachings, while centered on "love one another," also touch on other subjects, but John is most focused on our having peace and coexistence within the realm of believers. It is the confidence of our faith that seals the bond among believers

This improves our ability to recognize other believers. One of John's goals is to strengthen our communion. If we spot other Christians easily, and not have to wade through a maze of contradictory behavior and attitudes to develop a relationship, it makes for *better* relationships. We can, in a sense, jump right into our fellowship with them. Realizing others share our views and our standards enhances how we relate. With this tool we have *individual* reassurance and solidify group bonding.

> *he who says, "I know Him," and does not keep His commandments, is a liar, and the truth is not in him.*
>
> *1ˢᵗ John 2:4*

John starts his practical application with verse 3. And he wastes no words, cuts no one any slack. In a modification of his "if … then" syllogism, John flatly states if one says they "know" Christ but their life is not showing how they keep His commandments, then actions speak louder than words; they are lying and *don't* know Jesus.

Paul, writing in Romans, confirms the essentially dishonest nature of mankind.

> *[…] Indeed, let God be true but every man a liar. As it is written: "That You may be justified in Your words, And may overcome when You are judged."*
>
> *Romans 3:4*

Paul contrasts the absolute validity of everything we hear from God with the likelihood that most of what humans utter will be false.

Paul's quote is from Psalms 51, David's great cry of repentance. The essence of Paul's thinking is better grasped in the full context of the passage:

Have mercy upon me, O God, According to Your loving-kindness; According to the multitude of Your tender mercies, Blot out my transgressions.

Wash me thoroughly from my iniquity, And cleanse me from my sin.

For I acknowledge my transgressions, And my sin is always before me.

Against You, You only, have I sinned, And done this evil in Your sight-That You may be found just when You speak, And blameless when You judge.

Psalm 51:1–4 [emphasis added]

Examining the verses this way clarifies that the "You" relates to God, not to humanity. The purpose of Paul's quote is to affirm the integrity of the Almighty and reinforce the contrast between His constancy and our vagaries.

God's view of mankind is a level one; all societal hierarchies are flattened out. No one's social status places us in higher esteem than another. We all stand in the need of forgiveness, but once we accept the grace He offers, once more we are all equal, all His children. In Paul's ministry this was significant because it enabled him to show Gentiles of their need for salvation. For John (and others) focusing on the Jews, this concept solidified the universality of Christ's call for repentance.

But whoever keeps His word, truly the love of God is perfected in him. By this we know that we are in Him.

1John 2:5

"*Whoever.*" That pronoun steps out and says, "If your life is clear evidence to others, then we can be assured you are a believer." Again, John applies his "if ... then" format to make this statement. In this case it is a measurable action that communicates a fact, without the fact having to be trumpeted.

"At that day you will know that I am in My Father, and you in Me, and I in you.

"he who has My commandments and keeps them, it is he who loves Me. And he who loves Me will be loved by My Father, and I will love him and manifest Myself to him."

... said [...], "If anyone loves Me, he will keep My word; and My Father will love him, and We will come to him and make Our home with him.

John 14:21,23

In his Gospel, John recorded Christ's reassurance of this concept. The LORD'S sentence structure as translated into English is cumbersome, but the intent is affirmation through repetition. The real clue to Jesus' thought is conveyed in verse 23: *"If anyone <u>loves</u> Me ... "* The Greek form of "love" denotes a constant or repeated action, a continuous process, or habit. This rules out someone who only exhibits flashes of obedience and faithfulness to God; if the majority of the time their behavior does not reflect Jesus, they are not part of the flock. Conversely, one who may slip or stumble is a part of the kingdom, not to be disqualified by a single act or misstep. The key is the *continuous process or habit.* The verb form of *"keep"* is imperative, and is better translated *"you will keep,"* denoting an ongoing activity. John will repeatedly say it is the **lifestyle** that communicates the commitment. A **lifestyle** is something we do all the time.

Breaking down the John 14 passage, we see those who have God's commandments taught to them and keep them

Are loved,
One who loves Christ,
Will be loved in return by Him,
Will reveal Christ in their lives.

But whoever keeps His word, truly the love of God is perfected in him. By this we know that we are in Him.

1ˢᵗ John 2:5

John 14:21,23 again is the definition of "whoever." Don't get discouraged by "perfected." No one, no human, will ever be perfected as Christ was perfected. Here the meaning is ethical and spiritual maturity, completion, and successful conclusion. This is beautifully illustrated by the dialogue between Christ and the Samaritan woman. Her "perfection" was recognition of a man of God greater than Jacob. She convinced her neighbors and those of that little village became "perfected."

> *Then the woman of Samaria said to Him, "How is it that You, being a Jew, ask a drink from me, a Samaritan woman?" For Jews have no dealings with Samaritans.*
>
> *Jesus answered and said to her, "If you knew the gift of God, and who it is who says to you, "Give Me a drink," you would have asked Him, and he would have given you living water."*
>
> *The woman said to Him, "Sir, You have nothing to draw with, and the well is deep. Where then do You get that living water?*
>
> *"Are You greater than our father Jacob, who gave us the well, and drank from it himself, as well as his sons and his livestock?"*
>
> *Jesus answered and said to her, "Whoever drinks of this water will thirst again,*
>
> *"but whoever drinks of the water that I shall give him will never thirst. But the water that I shall give him will become in him a fountain of water springing up into everlasting life."*
>
> *The woman said to Him, "Sir, give me this water, that I may not thirst, nor come here to draw."*
>
> *Jesus said to her, "Go, call your husband, and come here."*

The woman answered and said, "I have no husband." Jesus said to her, "You have well said, 'I have no husband,'

"for you have had five husbands, and the one whom you now have is not your husband; in that you spoke truly."

The woman said to Him, "Sir, I perceive that You are a prophet.

"Our fathers worshiped on this mountain, and you Jews say that in Jerusalem is the place where one ought to worship."

Jesus said to her, "Woman, believe Me, the hour is coming when you will neither on this mountain, nor in Jerusalem, worship the Father.

"You worship what you do not know; we know what we worship, for salvation is of the Jews.

"But the hour is coming, and now is, when the true worshipers will worship the Father in spirit and truth; for the Father is seeking such to worship Him.

"God is Spirit, and those who worship Him must worship in spirit and truth."

The woman said to Him, "I know that Messiah is coming" (who is called Christ). "When he comes, he will tell us all things."

Jesus said to her, "I who speak to you am he."

And at this point His disciples came, and they marveled that he talked with a woman; yet no one said, "What do You seek?" or, "Why are You talking with her?"

The woman then left her water pot, went her way into the city, and said to the men,

"Come, see a Man who told me all things that I ever did. Could this be the Christ?"

Then they went out of the city and came to Him.

In the meantime His disciples urged Him, saying, "Rabbi, eat."

But he said to them, "I have food to eat of which you do not know."

Therefore the disciples said to one another, "Has anyone brought Him anything to eat?"

Jesus said to them, "My food is to do the will of Him who sent Me, and to finish His work.

"Do you not say, "There are still four months and then comes the harvest?" Behold, I say to you, lift up your eyes and look at the fields, for they are already white for harvest!

"And he who reaps receives wages, and gathers fruit for eternal life, that both he who sows and he who reaps may rejoice together.

"For in this the saying is true: "One sows and another reaps."

"I sent you to reap that for which you have not labored; others have labored, and you have entered into their labors."

And many of the Samaritans of that city believed in Him because of the word of the woman who testified, "he told me all that I ever did."

So when the Samaritans had come to Him, they urged Him to stay with them; and he stayed there two days.

And many more believed because of His own word.

John 4:9–41

This extended quote provides clarity to what the Jews (in this case, the Samaritans) were expecting in a Messiah. Jesus gently corrects that perception, and opens up an entirely new perspective on His purpose. Its refreshing guidance frees many souls locked into a despairing concept. It seals the teaching that evidence of atonement for sin is not reflected in the ritual performed but in the life exhibited. Jesus' teaching explains such a life is greater and more complete than any boastful claim or declaration by a priest. Being "in Christ" and living "in Christ" means we have achieved the "perfection" of His spirit living and totally controlling everything we do.

Much is said about "keeping the law" and the impossibility of doing so. Much is taught that evangelical Christians are free of the Law, that it is has served its purpose (which was to draw attention to the necessity for a sacrifice satisfying all the Mosaic requirements.) Adherence to the Law; in this teaching, is not necessary or even desirable. But knowledge and conformance to the Law encourages an understanding of God's nature and character. We seek to deepen our friendships by getting to know acquaintances better; we want to know about their hobbies; we try to see issues the way they do. This is no different from the manner in which we should want to grow our relationship with the LORD. Of course, we learn these things by studying His word, and prayer time with Him. As we acquire more and more wisdom about His nature, the more we implement modeling Him in our living. *It is the relationship He seeks, not the adherence.*

> *he who says he abides in Him ought himself also to walk just as [H]e walked.*
>
> *1ˢᵗ John 2:6*

This is a lot of pronouns, and with the trend in modern Bible translations not to capitalize the Almighty's pronouns, it could be confusing and redundant.

The first "he" is that individual in whom Christ abides.

"Abide in Me, and I in you. As the branch cannot bear fruit of itself, unless it abides in the vine, neither can you, unless you abide in Me."

John 15:4 [emphasis added]

The one abiding in Jesus is the one who acknowledges Christ and establishes that relationship.

"Him" is Jesus. The Apostle is reiterating what Jesus as saying; if you claim an association with the Savior, then it will be (not *must, should,* or *could be*) manifested in our living. In the Gospel, John reports Christ's instructions; in his letter John is establishing the standard for judging faithfulness to the instructions.

The use of "abide" is difficult to grasp as it applies to faith. In our usual concept *abide* means "put up with, stand for, bear, stomach, take, tolerate." It connotes a forbearance bordering on having to accept something we would prefer not to accept. Strong defines it as

> **Meno** (men'-o); #: 3306 –to remain, abide in reference to place (to sojourn, tarry; not to depart, to continue to be present, to be held, kept, continually); in reference to time (to continue to be, not to perish, to last, endure, of persons, to survive, live); in reference to state or condition (to remain as one, not to become another or different); to wait for, await one.

This communicates more of an allegiance. Understanding it in such a sense clarifies the point: "Abiding" with Jesus cements the connection between believer and Savior. That unity produces the "fruit," or outward evidence of a Christian life communicating to others where our hearts are. Now, the "walking as He walked" is easier to understand, and provides us the encouragement for living because (note this!) *the abiding is bi-lateral!* We are loyal and faithful to Christ, and He is just as loyal and faithful to us. The flow is in both directions. Knowing that makes the burden of living a Spirit-filled life less burdensome and much more natural.

The verb tense of "walk" connotes a continual, repeated, and constant action. This figurative striding is a moving ahead freely, in any direction, It is constant movement. It takes place in all circumstances and in every instance of our lives. God does not intend our existence to be static. Living is a continuous series of incidents requiring a response from us. Failure to react is the same as accepting a defeat.

Reliance on God's guidance is not an easy habit to form, but once established, we marvel at how we managed without it before. There is no fear; there is no need to hide or desire to control. We no longer flee from situations, whether we felt inadequate to face the issue or it was a matter we wished to avoid. A life totally controlled by God is a life of unimaginable ease. When the challenges come, and they do come, there is no anxiety about how to meet them. In a true "auto pilot" manner, we delegate control of our responses to Christ since he knows His plans for us and the direction in which we ought to go. Doubts recede and confidence soars. Soon, because of the ease with which we have confronted challenges, we begin to seek out new challenges. It is an endless cycle, one constantly spinning wider and wider around every aspect of our life.

But do not misunderstand. The worst disappointment to new Christians is the continuance of problems and trials. Jesus never promised us an absence from them; He did reassure us when the bad times come, we will have the strength, wisdom and guidance to handle them. It is not the dearth of struggles in our lives that makes the difference; it is the supernatural ability given us to deal with them,

The Apostle Peter also comments on this:

> *For to this you were called, because Christ also suffered for us, leaving us an example, that you should follow His steps:*

> *1ˢᵗ Peter 2:21*

Taking this passage apart, we find several reasons why we should follow Jesus Christ. First, we were "called" to that task. "Called" means we were invited to do the job. What greater honor than to be personally and individually sought out and invited by the LORD God Almighty? Would anyone refuse such a summons?

43

Christ suffered gruesome punishment and degradation on our behalf. Like the popular Christian song, "He took the blows, and like a rose was crushed" so we wouldn't have to suffer the same fate. We deserved it; He didn't.

Jesus' life was a model for us. In His every action was a guide for our behavior. Using it as a compass, we could find our way through the tangle of confusion and frustration and fear of everyday life.

All of this leads to the inevitable conclusion we have no other choice but to become a follower of Christ. Yet the beauty and wonder of God's salvation is that we *can* choose *not to do so*; we are not programmed robots. The gift of "free will" permits us to walk away from the offer of eternal life. But who wants the alternative?

The total sense of verse 6 is not that one who abides in Christ *should* behave as Christ, but **will** present that kind of life to the world. It is not a matter of electing. When we are absolutely committed to Jesus, our lifestyle broadcasts it. We follow His new commandments.

The Commandment – 1st John 2:7-9

There was an older commandment.

> *"You shall not take vengeance, nor bear any grudge against the children of your people, but <u>you shall love your neighbor as yourself</u>: I am the Lord.*

***Leviticus 19:18* [Emphasis added]**

Sound familiar? That is the original version of the "golden rule" Christ preaches in the Sermon on the Mount in Matthew 5 and 6. The "new" commandment from Jesus is His living example of it. Our faith in Him empowers us to keep the commandment. He also gave this commandment a new motive. No longer should we behave this way to defend ourselves, but instead because we want to. It is now our goal, our driving force for life. Because He has done it, we can do it, and we want to be more like Him in every way we can. Understanding how this becomes *the force* in our lives uncomplicates the faith of our lives.

> *Brethren, I write no new commandment to you, but an old commandment which you have had from the beginning. The old commandment is the word which you heard from the beginning.*

1ˢᵗ John 2:7

John admits what he is writing is not new. It has been taught since the dawn of creation by God's prophets, messengers, and now His Son. It is familiar to us, and it was well known in Christ's time. This makes not heeding it all the more inexcusable. Knowing the commandment, even in its stricter form as Jesus applies it, the people of Israel should have accepted it. What made Christ's amplification of it so difficult to accept was He now extends it to mental and spiritual attitudes, not just physical application.

> *Again, a new commandment I write to you, which thing is true in Him and in you, because the darkness is passing away, and the true light is already shining.*

> *1ˢᵗ John 2:8*

This new way of life is an imperative because now the lesson has been taught *in person* and *face-to-face* to the believers of John's time. They could not dismiss it as simply the teachings of someone claiming to be anointed by God; *this <u>was</u> God speaking to them.*

> *"A new commandment I give to you, that you love one another; as I have loved you, that you also love one another.*

> *John 13:34*

Christ Himself called it a "new" commandment.

> *"You shall not take vengeance, nor bear any grudge against the children of your people, but you shall love your neighbor as yourself: I am the Lord.*

> *Leviticus 19:18*

Take the "old commandment" apart. Don't seek revenge for the wrongs done to you. Put aside any feeling of resentment you have against those who have wronged you or your family. The solution is understood though not stated; *I, the LORD, will handle the punishment.* Our responsibility is to extend to those around you, your neighbors, the same kindness, and consideration you want showered on you. The *"I am the LORD"* phrase seals the charge; there should be no questioning. Its performance is not an option. God says so, and we should do so.

The difficulty the 1ˢᵗ century Jews had with Jesus' teaching was how He expanded it.

> *"You have heard that it was said, "You shall love your neighbor and hate your enemy."*

"But I say to you, love your enemies, bless those who curse you, do good to those who hate you, and pray for those who spitefully use you and persecute you,

"that you may be sons of your Father in heaven; for he makes His sun rise on the evil and on the good, and sends rain on the just and on the unjust.

"For if you love those who love you, what reward have you? Do not even the tax collectors do the same?

"And if you greet your brethren only, what do you do more than others? Do not even the tax collectors do so?

"Therefore you shall be perfect, just as your Father in heaven is perfect.

Matthew 5:43-48

Suddenly the commandment stretches beyond how to react to mistreatment. Suddenly it is spreads to heart attitudes, not just action. Jesus gives us a standard that stretches beyond response but to mindset. Believers now were being held accountable for those secret thoughts kept hidden in hearts. And it is so true. How can we claim to love our sisters and brothers when we harbor, deep inside, a feeling of distaste or distrust? How can we be expected to serve totally when we resent having to do some things?

John's teaching in 1st John is becoming clearer and more precise. Attitude equals action. Action reflects attitude. Attitude must demonstrate claim. Those with discerning spirits can tell when the behavior is only for show. And the danger, the awful threat to the reputation of Christianity, today as well as in the 1st Century, is "believers" are not representing the "beliefs." "Love one another, but sit in the back of the bus," those not truly filled with Christ's love say.

This is the salient point John pounds away at over and over again in 1st John. For followers of Christ to have *any* credibility in the world, they *must behave and think differently*. What they do and how they do it must be radically dissimilar from non-believers. Without that stamp of uniqueness, a Christian is no different from the heathen.

It is not to claim a distinction that John urges this approach; it is to spread the news of the saving grace of Jesus Christ. The reward for Christians is not in the number they bring into the kingdom, but the manner in which they live their lives representing God's standards. Soul-winning is best achieved by example, not by preaching. To the unsaved, an extraordinary life is more powerful than a sermon. "Show me ***how to live*** and I will live that way; don't you tell me how to live and then you live a different way. I will not be interested in what you have to say then."

On one occasion Jesus is asked to cite the greatest commandment of God, the one to which everyone should adhere. He answered,

> *"And you shall love the Lord your God with all your heart, with all your soul, with all your mind, and with all your strength." This is the first commandment.*
>
> *"And the second, like it, is this: "You shall love your neighbor as yourself." There is no other commandment greater than these."*

> *Mark 12:30-31*

If the Son of God considers caring for each other to be the second in line then surely we ought to consider it as a major linchpin of our living. A simple relational directive is touted as the key to kingdom living.

To be certain we've not misrepresented Jesus' teaching,

> *So he answered and said, "You shall love the Lord your God with all your heart, with all your soul, with all your strength, and with all your mind," and "your neighbor as yourself." "*
>
> *And he said to him, "You have answered rightly; do this and you will live."*

> *Luke 10:27-28*

There were those in the First Century who had not heard the Gospels, or were not witnesses or didn't hear accounts of Jesus' ministry from those who had seen it. But the Apostle Paul wrote to them and for them, and he made certain they understood what Christ was teaching.

> *For you, brethren, have been called to liberty; only do not use liberty as an opportunity for the flesh, but through love serve one another.*
>
> *For all the law is fulfilled in one word, even in this: "You shall love your neighbor as yourself."*
>
> *But if you bite and devour one another, beware lest you be consumed by one another!*
>
> *I say then: Walk in the Spirit, and you shall not fulfill the lust of the flesh.*
>
> *For the flesh lusts against the Spirit, and the Spirit against the flesh; and these are contrary to one another, so that you do not do the things that you wish.*
>
> **Galatians 5:13-17**

Some grasp principles only when portrayed to them as what **not** to do. So, in His infinite wisdom, the LORD had James write

> *My brethren, do not hold the faith of our Lord Jesus Christ, the Lord of glory, with partiality.*
>
> *For if there should come into your assembly a man with gold rings, in fine apparel, and there should also come in a poor man in filthy clothes,*
>
> *and you pay attention to the one wearing the fine clothes and say to him, "You sit here in a good place," and say to the poor man, "You stand there," or, "Sit here at my footstool,"*
>
> *have you not shown partiality among yourselves, and become judges with evil thoughts?*
>
> *Listen, my beloved brethren: Has God not chosen the poor of this world to be rich in faith and heirs of the kingdom which he promised to those who love Him?*

But you have dishonored the poor man. Do not the rich oppress you and drag you into the courts?

Do they not blaspheme that noble name by which you are called?

If you really fulfill the royal law according to the Scripture, "You shall love your neighbor as yourself," you do well;

but if you show partiality, you commit sin, and are convicted by the law as transgressors.

James 2:1-9

This tenet is not solely a theology of John's; it is a basic building block of Christian living. Peter and Paul both pound it home in their epistles. Without a clear acceptance of it, any practice of faith that falls short of it is not a valid faith. Nothing would be more disastrous than for an individual to think they are on the right path and actually not be. Those being understood, look further at these scriptural bases.

Let love be without hypocrisy. Abhor what is evil. Cling to what is good.

Romans 12:9 [emphasis added]

Since you have purified your souls in obeying the truth through the Spirit in sincere love of the brethren, love one another fervently with a pure heart,

having been born again, not of corruptible seed but incorruptible, through the word of God which lives and abides forever,

because "All flesh is as grass, And all the glory of man as the flower of the grass. The grass withers, And its flower falls away,

But the word of the Lord endures forever." Now this is the word which by the gospel was preached to you.

1 Peter 1:22-25

Paul defines for us the purpose of the new covenant:

Now the purpose of the commandment is love from a pure heart, from a good conscience, and from sincere faith,

from which some, having strayed, have turned aside to idle talk,

desiring to be teachers of the law, understanding neither what they say nor the things which they affirm.

1ˢᵗ Timothy 1:5-7

The new covenant is "love." It is love from a heart that is undefiled by, or at least not controlled by, the sinfulness of the world. Love springs from a clear conscience, free of regrets or anxieties. Love is from a sincere faith centered on Christ and His atoning death alone. One who meets these criteria exhibits "love" without consciously working at it; love is a natural evidence of their commitment to Jesus and His new commandment.

In John 15:2 Christ reiterates His creation of the "new commandment" and He intends for us to be devoted to others – friend and foe alike – in the same manner He cares for us. His "new commandment" has no other purpose, no other hidden agenda; there is no bargaining involved ("You do this, and I'll do that"). Adhering to the "new commandment" brings you nothing but the joy of peaceful coexistence. The comfort you receive results from not having to strain to keep relationships on a positive plane. It flows naturally; it makes the yoke of daily living so much easier.

The joy is not temporary; with the assurance of Jesus' love, our figurative walk is in every area of our life. It is continuous, also; repeatedly and daily, even hourly if needed, we have the comfort of the ability to love others in the same way Christ has loved us. This seemingly superhuman capacity to extend love makes our lives distinctive. Not only do we feel and act differently, but the distinction is noticeable to others, and gives rise to opportunities to share our secret. And sharing Christ this way – as an explanation of why we live as we do – for many is easier than trying to witness with a trail of scripture references and prayers.

> *And walk in love, as Christ also has loved us and given Himself for us, an offering and a sacrifice to God for a sweet-smelling aroma.*

> *Ephesians 5:2*

So, if for no other purpose than evangelizing, the "new commandment" serves our savior. Evangelization is what we have been commanded to be about, and thus the "new commandment" becomes "***THE*** commandment."

> *Again, a new commandment I write to you, which thing is true in Him and in you, because the darkness is passing away, and the true light is already shining.*

> *1ˢᵗ John 2:8*

John emphasizes the veracity of his statements about the "new commandment" by proclaiming it is "true in Him and in you." God cannot, by His nature, associate with anything which is false. If He represents this commandment, then it must be a true commandment. John offers as evidence of the commandment's power by asserting "the darkness is passing away, and the true light is already shining." We must acknowledge the diminishing of the darkness because God has said it was so; what He says must be true. "Because" verifies that what is stated is in fact, fact. The woes and evils of everyday living may seem to contradict this, but it is the power of our faith that assures us.

In his novels about the hobbits and the power of the Ring, J.R.R. Tolkein uses the metaphor of darkness to represent the growing evil power of those wishing to secure the Ring for nefarious purposes. In our society today we perceive the expansion of the influence of satanic concepts like a gathering thunderstorm cloud. But what is biblical darkness?

Since His nature would not permit God to utter anything false, this statement in 2:8 by Christ must be true. Whatever "the darkness" was (or is) it is retreating because the "true light" is already here and shining. It may be circular logic, but nevertheless the presence of the true light proves the darkness is going away, and if both those conditions are met, then the new commandment of loving one another is being carried out.

The truth of the new commandment was first and abundantly in Him. The new law is, in some measure, written upon your hearts; God teaches you to love one another. *"Because"* (or since, or, for as much as) *"the darkness is past,"* the darkness of your prejudiced unconverted (whether Jewish or Gentile) minds, your deplorable ignorance of God and of Christ is now past. *"And the true light is already shining"* (v. 8); *"the light"* of evangelical revelation has shone with life and efficacy into your hearts; you have seen the excellency of Christian love, and you're the fundamental obligation to living that life fully. The more our darkness is past, and the gospel light shines unto us, the deeper should our subjection be to the commandments of our Lord, whether considered as old or new. Light should produce a suitable heat.

"Darkness" is ignorance of divine truth, man's sinful nature. It is the absence of light in a life. There is a lack of spiritual perception. It is anything earthly or demonic, or that is at enmity with God.

To further clarify the nature of "darkness" it may be helpful to review how scripture describes "the light."

> *Indeed he says, "It is too small a thing that You should be My Servant To raise up the tribes of Jacob, And to restore the preserved ones of Israel; I will also give You as a light to the Gentiles, That You should be My salvation to the ends of the earth."*

> **Isaiah 49:6**

The LORD tells Isaiah He will send a Servant who will restore Israel and who shall be the salvation of the Earth. He shall be a "light" to the Gentiles, showing them the path to reunion and communion with God. That "light" is the salvation of the world. The "light" is a guide.

> *"A new commandment I give to you, that you love one another; as I have loved you, that you also love one another.*
>
> *"By this all will know that you are My disciples, if you have love for one another."*
>
> *John 13:34-35*

The "light" of the commandment will confirm to believers they *are* the faithful and they will be assured of the path, the way, to salvation. The "true light" is already shining, and making the direction we should follow, the life we should live. It is clear to us; every step is illuminated by the glory of Jesus and the Holy Spirit in our hearts.

The commandment of 2:8 is new, and it is true and valid because the root and nature of it is in Jesus Christ and in us as Christians. The commandment is given because the evil of the world is being and will eventually be totally replaced by the power and majesty of God's kingdom.

> *he who says he is in the light, and hates his brother, is in darkness until now.*
>
> *1ˢᵗ John 2:9*

John is going to address this disparity four times in this epistle, each time with increasingly harsher judgment. Here, he simply says anyone who claims to be a Christian and yet harbors animosity towards another is not part of the fellowship.

Anyone who still does not love others is not a believer even though they claim to be. Paul says in 1 Corinthians 13:2 such a person is "nothing." Lacking love for others is a sign one is not living as one should, certainly not living as a follower of Jesus. Such a life is still controlled by the darkness of the world and its system.

Testing the Light – 1st John 2:10-14

This "test" is not infallible, but it is a major barometer. Since we are cautioned to *"judge not lest you be judged"* it is a reasonable measuring tool for ourselves. Harboring hatred or dislike for another should signal us we are not in the path of righteous living. It doesn't mean we've lost our salvation, but it ought to remind us of our attitudes. Just as we long for and appreciate the extension of grace to us, we need to be active is doing the same to those to whom we feel less than attracted. God has showered us with His grace; our earthly grace is as valuable.

> *he who loves his brother abides in the light, and there is no cause for stumbling in him.*
>
> *1ˢᵗ John 2:10*

Look in the next chapter of 1ˢᵗ John; the writer defines "he who loves"

> *We know that we have passed from death to life, because we love the brethren. he who does not love his brother abides in death*
>
> *1ˢᵗ John 3:14*

In uncomplicated English, we're living in the grace of Jesus when we love our brothers (and sisters). There may be no physical or visible mark on us when we accept Jesus as savior, but our attitude and behavior speaks loud and clear. That beam of love emanating from us is not only a beacon to others but it is a headlamp for our daily walk.

There may be shades of interpretation of what constitute a believer, but look at the Apostle Peter as the authority for who **is not** a believer. 2ⁿᵈ Peter 2:10 says those who walk according to the flesh (the world), walk in the lust of (and for) things which are unclean, those who despise authority (especially divine authority), who are presumptuous, self-willed and not afraid to speak ill of dignitaries might be unbelievers. Very few persons could exhibit that kind of life style and be mistaken as "Christians."

John offers reassurance at the end of verse 10. If you are not one of those living in darkness, you have nothing to fear; you will not knowingly be entrapped or drawn into sinfulness. Our very styles of living will protect us from falling. Even if we do slip, we know forgiveness is available and granted when we confess and repent (see Chapter 1, verses 6 and 7). And personal experience should teach us repentance need only be accomplished once. If one enmeshes themselves with the Word of God, the Spirit thrives. A thriving Holy Spirit will direct us away from those areas which have proved detrimental to us in the past. Our walk becomes steadier and narrower.

But many Christians today confine their scripture study to the pre-packaged devotionals so readily available. That is not how our study of God's Word should be. As a counselor once expressed it to me, "When you get hungry, do you go find someone who is a chef, and then eat what they have chewed up and then spit out of their mouths?" The answer is, of course, "No." What we want to do is to partake of the glorious fruit of the scripture, "chew" on it mentally, then swallow it and allow it to nourish our spiritual body.

John continues his identification of those in darkness and those in "the light."

> *But he who hates his brother is in darkness and walks in darkness, and does not know where he is going, because the darkness has blinded his eyes.*

> *1ˢᵗ John 2:11*

One who hates his brother (or sister) is
    In darkness
        Still is in darkness
            Walks and lives in darkness
They don't know how to achieve righteousness or how to reach heaven because they have allowed the darkness to screen their spiritual eyes. This briefly summarizes the state of one with hate in their heart. The shading of spiritual eyes is a willful, intentional one; it has to be, because the glory and majesty of the God's creation is all around us.

One must consciously reject the power of the LORD in the world; it naturally overwhelms us. The turning of the back on such magnificence must therefore be premeditated and deliberate. Such a rejection of God results in life in the darkness.

How we relate to others reflects our walk with Christ and our life in Christ. Since light and darkness are bitter enemies, they will always be in contention, just as love and hate will be. The strength we exhibit by confession and repentance reveal our determination to seek out and <u>stay</u> in the light. Not admitting our failures, refusing to seek forgiveness for them, and not turning in a new direction, confirms how utterly blind we are. Such living is living in darkness.

Verse 12 of this chapter may be the start of an early Christian hymn, psalm, or praise song. Its physical structure on the early copies of the pages indicates it has special significance to the writer. John directs comments to each of three different levels of spiritual growth levels in believers. These are "spiritual ages," not chronological ages. Since a distinction of a maturing Christian is continual growth, none of the labels is meant to be a permanent one; everyone should be striving to move to the highest level, but there is no shame in being at a lower one *unless one is <u>not</u> making a diligent effort to grow.* John's comments are motivational, not condemning. There is also an element of *warning*, letting the readers know there will be challenges and temptations ahead.

> *I write to you, little children,*
>
> *Because your sins are forgiven you for His name's sake.*
>
> *I write to you, fathers,*
>
> *Because you have known Him who is from the beginning.*
>
> *I write to you, young men,*
>
> *Because you have overcome the wicked one.*
>
> *I write to you, little children,*
>
> *Because you have known the Father.*

I have written to you, fathers,

Because you have known Him who is from the beginning.

I have written to you, young men,

Because you are strong, and the word of God abides in you,

And you have overcome the wicked one.

1ˢᵗ John 2:12–14

John's "little children" are those who are new to the faith, "baby Christians" we call them today. They are filled with exuberance and enthusiasm for their new found freedom in Christ. But they are only able to comprehend basic doctrine; complex issues are beyond them. Paul characterizes them as only being able to digest the "milk" of the faith, not yet grown-up enough to get nourishment from the "meat" of the faith. Again, there is no shame in being at this stage; everyone has to begin someplace.[9] The intent is to develop a more advanced Christ-like life.

John's comment to the little children first is to reassure them of their forgiveness, the matter that is most precious at that stage of their walk. They are glad to be freed from the burden of sin. The verb tense used in "forgiven" connotes they were forgiven at one time and place, but the action continues onward; they still are forgiven. It follows them. It is always available.

[...]But you were washed, but you were sanctified, but you were justified in the name of the Lord Jesus and by the Spirit of our God.

1ˢᵗ Corinthians 6:11

Paul had earlier written of the assurance of this forgiveness. It is total, it is complete and it is authentic.

"Fathers" are the next level of mature believers. They have been in the faith a longer time, longer at least by the standards of the brief history of Christianity. These are the ones, both female and male (though John uses masculine pronouns, it should be understood he speaks of both genders), who recognize the full revelation of Jesus' nature and the power of the Holy Spirit. They grasp the meaning of His life from birth, through ministry and miracles, to death and resurrection. They anticipate His return and reign. Forgiveness is for them a reassurance, not a concern.

"Young men" are the believers in the middle – not freshly born again, but not having lived the faith long enough to have the wisdom of the fathers. They can claim victory in that they have accepted Jesus Christ as LORD. They begin to see the transforming power of Him in their lives. As they grow, the revelation of spiritual concepts is exciting to them. On faith they have received:

> *For you did not receive the spirit of bondage again to fear, but you received the Spirit of adoption by whom we cry out, "Abba, Father."*
>
> *The Spirit Himself bears witness with our spirit that we are children of God,*
>
> *and if children, then heirs-heirs of God and joint heirs with Christ, if indeed we suffer with Him, that we may also be glorified together.*
>
> *Romans 8:15–17*

"The Spirit of Adoption" is exclusively a Pauline term, describing a relationship that grants us absolute access to God through the Christ. We are no longer separated from the Creator because of our sinfulness; that has been cleansed on our profession of faith.

> *And he said, "Abba, Father, all things are possible for You. Take this cup away from Me; nevertheless, not what I will, but what You will."*
>
> *Mark 14:36*

If Jesus can cry out to His Father like this, then we can cry out to Him as well. And with the mystifying intermingling of the relationship among the members of the Trinity, there is no distinction at all to whom we are praying and communicating. We need no special status to seek direction or ask favor. The first thing we get upon adoption is *equality*. This equality assures us of our worth and value to the LORD; we are as significant to Him as is His own Son. It is this value that should reassure us of our standing with God. Each of us is the same as every other believer. Paul's reference to "neither Jew nor Gentile" affirms the playing field has been leveled. No believer has any advantage over another.

> *Even to them I will give in My house And within My walls a place and a name Better than that of sons and daughters; I will give them an everlasting name That shall not be cut off.*

> *Isaiah 56:5*

The next gifts given us are a "house," ultimately that mansion in heaven Jesus is preparing for us, but think of it as permanence and coexistence. Within those walls we are granted a "place," a standing which implies responsibility and recognition. God gives us a "name," meaning we have individuality. We are given an inheritance, one that is permanent and cannot be revoked or rescinded, *no matter how we may fail in the future*. Children can be written out of wills, but God promises He'll never forsake us or disown us once we come into His house.

Now about that "everlasting name." Names are significant in the Bible. Often their meanings are clues to the character of the person. In some cases parents gave a child a name reflective of their aspirations or expectations; these sometimes become self-fulfilling prophecies. The implication for Christians about an "everlasting name" is that name being written in the Lamb's Book of Life that is opened and studied at Judgment, according to John's Revelation. Our name is our "passport" into eternity with Jesus.

Lastly, Isaiah confirms we are "not cut off." We are part of the heavenly community. The kingdom to which we belong is an eternal kingdom. Our citizenship is assured. There may be times in our minds when we doubt we are saved, but there is never any doubt or question of it with God. Having performed the work of salvation on the cross, and our having accepting that work as being done for us seals the deal.

We're in, and that's it. Isaiah confirms it by stating it so plainly and flatly. And remember Isaiah's revelation was hundreds of years before the birth of Jesus.

Paul's use of the term "heirs" in Romans 8:15–17 indicates confirmation of our acceptance into the family of God. "Heirs" are those who receive a promise or a promised thing. In Messianic usage, it is one who receives his allotted possession by right of sonship, one who has acquired or obtained the portion allotted to him.

> *By faith he dwelt in the land of promise as in a foreign country, dwelling in tents with Isaac and Jacob, the heirs with him of the same promise;*
>
> *Hebrews 11:9*

This citation in Hebrews defines the inheritance granted to Abraham and relates it, in the context of Hebrews, to that which believers receive from Jesus. It is tangible and it is shared; what is given to us is ours <u>and</u> it is Christ's. We hold heavenly citizenship jointly with our Savior. Abraham was a stranger in the land promised to him and his seed, dwelling as did Isaac and Jacob, in tents, yet trusting the promise of God that one day he would live in a permanent home. So we live on Earth but anticipate that day when we will move to our permanent heavenly dwelling place.

As Paul delivers his conversion testimony in Acts 26, in verse 18 he repeats the concept that those who have accepted Christ as redeemer are comparable to the early Hebrews who because of the faith of their fathers (Abraham, Isaac, and Jacob) were granted the possession of the Promised Land four hundred years later.

How do we *know* we are "joint heirs?" Paul reassures us in his letter to the Philippians.

> *For to you it has been granted on behalf of Christ, not only to believe in Him, but also to suffer for His sake, having the same conflict which you saw in me and now hear is in me.*
>
> *Philippians 1:29–30*

The concept seems a bit contradictory; we follow by faith and anticipate great rewards and blessings, but before we can get them we have to endure hardships and anguish. This is a purifying process of faith—a testing, a trial. How we handle the rough spots shows how deep our convictions are. This flows along with John's contention that one claiming to have Christ in their heart will reflect Him in their life.

John follows the Jewish literary tradition by repeating verses 12 and 13 in verse 14 with some minor variations, primarily for emphasis and not to introduce any new concepts. The mature believers have known its essence from the beginning. The young believers have become "strong," faithful in the pursuit of the light of Christ. Their hearts are completely devoted to Him. That dedication is reflected in their daily living. They have *rejected* Satan by *accepting* Jesus. Their faithfulness is the evidence of their victory. It is a never-ending cycle; their overcoming of evil strengthens their faith and that is then evidenced in their life, and the confirmation of their life gives them the power to continue to be victorious.

These passages, 2:12–14, is John's way of reassurance of the total, complete and absolute forgiveness of sins. God is changeless, and his readers acceptance of Jesus' gift of grace guarantees their eternal security. Not only is the repetition an effort to comfort, but it provides believers with a means of maintaining their sensitivity to the work of God in their life. Reflection on each of the levels John identifies provides Christians the basis for each day"s challenges. Not only is this passage one of praise, but what a marvelous hymn of encouragement!

Living in the World – 1st John 2:15-17

Do not love the world or the things in the world. If anyone loves the world, the love of the Father is not in him.

1ˢᵗ John 2:15

John returns to the traditional format of letter writing as he resumes his basic instructions for living the Christian life. In its most simple form, John tells us not to be devoted to the carnal ways of the world. There is a clear distinction between a life lived in the natural, humanistic, unsaved way and the pattern of living for the Christian. John continues to assert the two lifestyles are incompatible; they cannot co-exist in a believer. If one finds the way of the world more attractive, more convenient, more pleasing, they do not deeply possess the Holy Spirit and are not entirely devoted to Christ as their Savior.

Grace to you and peace from God the Father and our Lord Jesus Christ ,who gave Himself for our sins, that he might deliver us from this present evil age, according to the will of our God and Father, to whom be glory forever and ever. Amen.

Galatians 1:3–5

Paul, writing to the church in Galatia, is just as dogmatic. In this passage he points out Jesus' sacrificial death was to transport us from society. The meaning behind "evil" means bad, of a bad nature or condition; in a physical sense: diseased or blind; in an ethical sense: evil and wicked. So Paul isn't talking about just an unpleasant circumstance, he's pointing his finger at a society that is sick and depraved, much as our own current society is. The surprising thing we can carry from this passage is not the message, but the setting. It is hard to imagine the world of Paul's time was worse than what we see around us today.

A favorite sermon topic among preachers for centuries has been the impossibility of being "double-minded" and claiming to be a follower of Jesus. Here is where that concept gets its basis:

> *"No one can serve two masters; for either he will hate the one and love the other, or else he will be loyal to the one and despise the other. You cannot serve God and mammon.*

> *Matthew 6:24*

When John heard this preached, it seared into his brain to the point that it became his rallying cry, the cry we hear throughout this letter. Jesus was saying one cannot legitimately *work for* (to be a slave, serve, do service of a nation in subjection to other nations; metaphorically, to obey, submit to; in a good sense, to yield obedience; of those who become slaves to some base power, to yield to, give one's self up to) God's kingdom <u>and</u> the world's system. The two are not compatible. It is against this dichotomy that John so strenuously teaches. And Christ reiterates the point in a number of his parables and sermons. We must make the decision; choosing to work for "the world" is not bad, it simply is not the *best* choice we could make.

By the way, for years I tried to puzzle out "mammon." Was it simply a quaint King James way of saying "mankind?" When I finally got serious about biblical study and began to use a concordance, I discovered the true definition. It means "treasure, riches (where it is personified and opposed to God)." That brings Jesus' teaching even sharper into focus because it characterizes precisely the ends of the spectrum, God is on one end, worldly goods and treasure on the other.

> *Pure and undefiled religion before God and the Father is this: to visit orphans and widows in their trouble, and to keep oneself unspotted from the world.*

> *James 1:27*

That makes it pretty clear if one is to live a religious and righteous life, one must not be contaminated by the world. And note that James considers "religious" work is to be for widows and orphans, the two classes of citizens in his society who had absolutely no influence. Both were considered to be burdens shunted aside as quickly as possible.

James doesn't stop in his first chapter.

> *Adulterers and adulteresses! Do you not know that friendship with the world is enmity with God? Whoever therefore wants to be a friend of the world makes himself an enemy of God.*

> **James 4:4**

"Making friends" with these people absolutely doesn't fit into the criteria of being one of God's elect. This class of sinner was to be punished by stoning to death, not exactly a pleasant way to die, but it was the prescribed mode of execution (Exodus 19:13; Leviticus 20:27; Joshua 7:25; Luke 20:6; Acts 7:58; 14:5). The witnesses, (of whom there were needed at least two) were required to cast the first stone (Deuteronomy 13:9 following; John 8:7). If these failed to cause death, the bystanders proceeded to complete the sentence, whereupon the body was to be suspended until sunset (Deuteronomy 21:23).

One should understand the "worldliness" taught against in scripture means the *acceptance* of society's standards; simply living in its wretchedness is not grounds for condemnation. Many have scurried off to monastic living because they were unable to endure the negative influences of the world and they sought the safety of isolation. The victory is not found in such abandonment but in triumphing over the misery of humanity.

John wants to be firm in what he considers "the world" so he writes

> *For all that is in the world-the lust of the flesh, the lust of the eyes, and the pride of life-is not of the Father but is of the world.*

> *1ˢᵗ John 2:16*

John views the world as the sinful use of those things God has created, using them in the wrong way, not the way they were intended to be used. He intentionally is referring to the negative influences *in* creation; he is not saying the design of mankind and the earth by God is bad. John's concern is the impact of living in a fallen world on believers.

"Lust" is the longing, the craving desire for that which is forbidden. In its proper use, man's desire should be for the things which are glorious and good. "The flesh" is our earthly nature. We should crave our heavenly nature. "The eyes" mean our faculty of knowing, of pursuing knowledge. The LORD did not create us to be ignorant. His intent was for us to search and explore to discover for ourselves the glories of His creation. "The pride of life" is an empty presumption trusting in our earthly abilities, and not in the power of Creator God. These corruptions, according to John, are not God's, but are from the world.

All the things God has created man has corrupted their use by his sinful nature. The marvelous creations of God have been turned to sinful purposes because of our fallen character. "The lust of the flesh" is the misapplied appetite for our most powerful needs and desires: food, intimacy (physical relationships), and recognition. These needs must be met for us to be healthy and productive. When they become selfish, an overwhelming obsession, when our humanness takes control of them, then they excite and inflame our passions. That passionate craving then draws us away from a right and proper relationship with Jesus.

The "lust of the eye" gets a bit more complicated. Here the danger is in what we can actually *see* and *what we can imagine*. Now the power of the capacity to think granted to us by The Creator can be turned to dark purposes. We must exercise self-control and discipline otherwise the gift of sight will be subverted and corrupted.

> *he who loves silver will not be satisfied with silver; Nor he who loves abundance, with increase. This also is vanity.*
>
> *When goods increase, They increase who eat them; So what profit have the owners Except to see them with their eyes?*
>
> **Ecclesiastes 5:10–11**

Wise Solomon writes those who seek after and worship riches will never be satisfied. The more one possesses the more potential for dissatisfaction it generates because there never seems to be enough of it to completely satisfy. John D. Rockefeller is said to have replied to the question how much money do you need to have to be happy, "One dollar more than I have."

God, in His mercy, has created many things pleasurable to behold. We're graced with glorious sunrises and sunsets, the dazzling stars, the majestic mountain peaks, and stately forests. Our human minds are never content with just what we can see; we want more. It is our responsibility, our duty, and our necessity, to understand we cannot claim it all. Controlling lust of the eye is difficult, but it is absolutely critical to living "in the world but not of the world."

"The pride of life" is claiming the vain glory of the world, a feeling of self-sufficiency, the joy we have in what "*we*" have attained without acknowledging it as the gift from our gracious heavenly father. It is a very dangerous attitude of trusting in the power of our "selves" and not trusting in the power of God. There should be pride in our accomplishments, and we should all strive to do the very best we can. Credit, though, needs to be given to God; we could not have performed as we have without the gifts and wisdom He has bestowed on us. If our victory is because of things we have learned, we must acknowledge it was His guidance that led us to the information we needed.

None of these attitudes represents the LORD; all of them need to be curtailed if we are to truly live as Christians.

> *And the world is passing away, and the lust of it; but he who does the will of God abides forever.*

> *1ˢᵗ John 2:17*

John doesn't have much hope in the social and political structure, the earthly design, the human nature, the manufactured contents, and the standards of this decadent "world." It has been judged already by the LORD because of its rejection of salvation. John offers the consolation, though, for those who do follow in Christ; they will live forever.

But this I say, brethren, the time is short, so that from now on even those who have wives should be as though they had none,

those who weep as though they did not weep, those who rejoice as though they did not rejoice, those who buy as though they did not possess,

and those who use this world as not misusing it. For the form of this world is passing away.

1ˢᵗ Corinthians 7:29–31

Paul agrees with John on the future of unsaved mankind. The teaching is absolutely universal as well as true. Scofield's commentary further explains the dismal future for the "world."

In the sense of the present world-system, the ethically bad sense of the word refers to the "order," "arrangement," under which Satan has organized the world of unbelieving mankind upon his cosmic principle of force, greed, selfishness, ambition, and pleasure. This world-system is imposing and powerful with armies and fleets; is often outwardly religious, scientific, cultured, and elegant; but, seething with national and commercial rivalries and ambitions, is upheld in any real crisis only by armed force, and is dominated by Satanic principles.

[...]"All flesh is as grass, And all the glory of man as the flower of the grass. The grass withers, And its flower falls away,

But the word of the Lord endures forever." Now this is the word which by the gospel was preached to you.

1ˢᵗ Peter 1:24–25

Peter affirms the judgment by quoting Solomon's final assessment from Ecclesiastes. Our hope, as believers, is in the antithesis to these gloom-and-doom statements: the eternal life offered and promised by God to those who do the work of Jesus.

The Last Hour – 1st John 2:18-20

Little children, it is the last hour; and as you have heard that the Antichrist is coming, even now many antichrists have come, by which we know that it is the last hour.

1ˢᵗ John 2:18

N ow, just as it was in John's lifetime, is a critical and dangerous time. We know it is because we see so much evidence of many who claim to be "the answer" (but they are not). John's contemporaries faced the same challenge. All those in the past, and all those who are "practicing" today, are precursors of the authentic antichrist. The repetition of the phrase "the last hour" emphasizes John's assessment that time is short.

"The antichrist, " is a being who is against Christ, a rival Christ. The word is used only by the apostle John. Referring to false teachers, he says, "Even now are there are many antichrists." In other passages the concept of the antichrist has been applied to the "little horn" of the "king of fierce countenance."

The ten horns are ten kings Who shall arise from this kingdom. And another shall rise after them; he shall be different from the first ones, And shall subdue three kings.

he shall speak pompous words against the Most High, Shall persecute the saints of the Most High, And shall intend to change times and law. Then the saints shall be given into his hand For a time and times and half a time.

Daniel 7:24–25

"And in the latter time of their kingdom, When the transgressors have reached their fullness, A king shall

arise, Having fierce features, Who understands sinister schemes.

His power shall be mighty, but not by his own power; he shall destroy fearfully, And shall prosper and thrive; he shall destroy the mighty, and also the holy people.

"Through his cunning he shall cause deceit to prosper under his rule; And he shall exalt himself in his heart. he shall destroy many in their prosperity. he shall even rise against the Prince of princes; But he shall be broken without human means.

Daniel 8:23–25

It has been applied also to the "false Christs" spoken of by our Lord:

"For many will come in My name, saying, "I am the Christ," and will deceive many. ...

"Therefore if you bring your gift to the altar, and there remember that your brother has something against you,

"leave your gift there before the altar, and go your way. First be reconciled to your brother, and then come and offer your gift.

Matthew 24:5, 23–24

Paul described the antichrist as the "man of sin:"

Let no one deceive you by any means; for that Day will not come unless the falling away comes first, and the man of sin is revealed, the son of perdition,

who opposes and exalts himself above all that is called God or that is worshiped, so that he sits as God in the temple of God, showing himself that he is God. ...

And then the lawless one will be revealed, whom the Lord will consume with the breath of His mouth and destroy with the brightness of His coming.

71

> *The coming of the lawless one is according to the working of Satan, with all power, signs, and lying wonders,*
>
> *and with all unrighteous deception among those who perish, because they did not receive the love of the truth, that they might be saved.*
>
> *2nd Thessalonians 2:3–4, 8–10*

John uses his exclusive term when describing the "beast from the sea" in his Revelation:

> *Then I stood on the sand of the sea. And I saw a beast rising up out of the sea, having seven heads and ten horns, and on his horns ten crowns, and on his heads a blasphemous name.*
> *...*
>
> *Then one of the seven angels who had the seven bowls came and talked with me, saying to me, "Come, I will show you the judgment of the great harlot who sits on many waters,*
>
> *"with whom the kings of the earth committed fornication, and the inhabitants of the earth were made drunk with the wine of her fornication."*
>
> *So he carried me away in the Spirit into the wilderness. And I saw a woman sitting on a scarlet beast which was full of names of blasphemy, having seven heads and ten horns.*
>
> *The woman was arrayed in purple and scarlet, and adorned with gold and precious stones and pearls, having in her hand a golden cup full of abominations and the filthiness of her fornication.*
>
> *And on her forehead a name was written: MYSTERY, BABYLON THE GREAT, THE MOTHER OF HARLOTS AND OF THE ABOMINATIONS OF THE EARTH.*

I saw the woman, drunk with the blood of the saints and with the blood of the martyrs of Jesus. And when I saw her, I marveled with great amazement.

But the angel said to me, "Why did you marvel? I will tell you the mystery of the woman and of the beast that carries her, which has the seven heads and the ten horns.

"The beast that you saw was, and is not, and will ascend out of the bottomless pit and go to perdition. And those who dwell on the earth will marvel, whose names are not written in the Book of Life from the foundation of the world, when they see the beast that was, and is not, and yet is.

"here is the mind which has wisdom: The seven heads are seven mountains on which the woman sits.

"There are also seven kings. Five have fallen, one is, and the other has not yet come. And when he comes, he must continue a short time.

"And the beast that was, and is not, is himself also the eighth, and is of the seven, and is going to perdition.

"The ten horns which you saw are ten kings who have received no kingdom as yet, but they receive authority for one hour as kings with the beast.

"These are of one mind, and they will give their power and authority to the beast.

"These will make war with the Lamb, and the Lamb will overcome them, for he is Lord of lords and King of kings; and those who are with Him are called, chosen, and faithful."

Then he said to me, "The waters which you saw, where the harlot sits, are peoples, multitudes, nations, and tongues.

"And the ten horns which you saw on the beast, these will hate the harlot, make her desolate and naked, eat her flesh and burn her with fire.

"For God has put it into their hearts to fulfill His purpose, to be of one mind, and to give their kingdom to the beast, until the words of God are fulfilled.

"And the woman whom you saw is that great city which reigns over the kings of the earth. "

Revelation 13:1; 17:1–18

John defines the antichrist in a manner leaving no doubt as to his intrinsic meaning, but exactly to whom he applies the appellation there is some vagueness. In 1st John 2:18 (the first appearance of the term) the apostle makes direct reference to the false Christs whose coming will mark the last days. Further down in the chapter (in verse 22) John says, "he is antichrist, that denies the Father and the Son;" and still more precisely, "every spirit that confesses not that Jesus Christ is come in the flesh is of antichrist." From his emphatic and repeated definitions it appears the intention of the apostle was to contest the errors of Cerinthus, the Docetae and the Gnostics on the subject of the Incarnation. (The Gnostics denied the union of the divine and human in Christ.) The first embodiment of the "spirit of the antichrist" was in Epiphanes but the complete fulfillment was reserved for the "last times."

Even though John is the only New Testament writer to use the specific term "Antichrist" the concept is found in other passages.

Let no one deceive you by any means; for that Day will not come unless the falling away comes first, and the man of sin is revealed, the son of perdition,

who opposes and exalts himself above all that is called God or that is worshiped, so that he sits as God in the temple of God, showing himself that he is God.

Do you not remember that when I was still with you I told you these things?

2nd Thessalonians 2:3–5

Paul writes to his congregation at Thessalonica to recall his teaching on the subject as events seem to be pointing towards the appearance of the evil one. Never one to mince words, Paul describes the individual as one not only soaked in sinfulness but who is doomed to an utter destruction of eternal misery in hell. This is not just a temporary loss of well-being; it is a circumstance of absolute condemnation.

Notice that Paul in verse 4 describes a scene that John witnesses later in his Revelation, the Antichrist going into the restored temple and proclaiming himself God and demanding the world's worship. Skeptics of the God-inspired nature of the Bible may say that John latched on to this seed of an idea from Paul's letter and used it in writing his Revelation. It is possible John may have heard Paul's letter; it was written 30 to 35 years before the Revelation, but remember that Paul had also been granted a peek behind the veil and was perhaps recording the same scenes John would witness later.

"For many will come in My name, saying, "I am the Christ," and will deceive many.

Matthew 24:5

"For false christs and false prophets will rise and show great signs and wonders to deceive, if possible, even the elect.

"See, I have told you beforehand.

"Therefore if they say to you, "Look, he is in the desert!" do not go out; or "Look, he is in the inner rooms!" do not believe it.

"For as the lightning comes from the east and flashes to the west, so also will the coming of the Son of Man be.

Matthew 24:24–28

Jesus taught his disciples privately about the last days. In this section of Matthew 24 He tells them there will be many who pretend to be the Christ in His second coming. These imposters will pose as priests and prophets (in today's culture, these would be evangelists and cult leaders). Their ability to perform miracles would be consistent with the power Satan and his followers have. When **the** antichrist truly does appear, believers will truly need to test what they see and hear as they make decisions on whom to follow.

John uses once more that affectionate term, "Little children." He uses a diminutive form emphasizing its warmth, identical to Jesus calling His disciples "children" on the beach the morning following His resurrection. One can picture a loving parent, opening arms encircling and enfolding a youngster, offering protection and comfort. For many years we"ve had on the wall in our home a charcoal drawing of an infant sitting in the palm of a giant hand, reaching upward with its arms to hug that which holds it; that image is precisely what I think of when I read John's use of "little children" in his writing.

> *And do this, knowing the time, that now it is high time*
> *to awake out of sleep; for now our salvation is nearer*
> *than when we first believed.*

> **Romans 13:11**

"The last hours" is a double-edge deadline to be feared and to be anticipated. The joy of it is that our salvation is now nearer at hand than when we first were saved. No one knows except the Father when Jesus will return but logic tells us that if He has not come back today, He could come tomorrow.

Paul also says this day would be the one when we would awaken out of our "spiritual sleep." Not all theologians adhere to the concept of "spiritual sleep" or "soul sleep." *Soul Sleep* says that when we die, our souls cease to function or "fall asleep," until the end of the world and our resurrection. Various religions have different understandings about exactly how soul sleep works, but in practical terms it would mean that the dead are not conscious in any way. It is my own personal interpretation of Paul's use of the term here to be figurative, referring to our inactive and passive faith, not any disposition of our souls. He is sounding a call to action, to righteous living, a restoration of our Christian behavior.

> *Now the Spirit expressly says that in latter times some will depart from the faith, giving heed to deceiving spirits and doctrines of demons,*
>
> *speaking lies in hypocrisy, having their own conscience seared with a hot iron,*
>
> *forbidding to marry, and commanding to abstain from foods which God created to be received with thanksgiving by those who believe and know the truth.*
>
> *1ˢᵗ Timothy 4:1–3*

Paul writes to his protégé Timothy of the Day of Judgment he foresees. His descriptions of the times when that will occur correspond to John's depiction of society as well. It will be a time when numerous believers will abandon their faith; they will have been deceived about the truth of living a Christian life. These desertions will not be a surprise to God; He knew from the day of creation who would remain steadfast and who would not.

These disaffected ones will deny the essential elements of the Christian faith. They will teach doctrines inspired by Satan in an effort to undermine the growing influence of devotion to Jesus Christ. They will try to lead away careless believers from the path of righteousness. Those not solidly grounded and not consistently practicing Christianity will be the targets and victims.

> *For they are spirits of demons, performing signs, which go out to the kings of the earth and of the whole world, to gather them to the battle of that great day of God Almighty.*
>
> *Revelation 16:14*

None other than the Apostle Peter joins in with suggestions of how to prepare for this fateful time:

But the end of all things is at hand; therefore be serious and watchful in your prayers.

And above all things have fervent love for one another, for "love will cover a multitude of sins."

1st Peter 4:7–8

It should not be considered a fault of the biblical writers that they misinterpreted their present age and were so certain the Second Coming was imminent. No doubt circumstances were unbelievably frightening for them; nothing like this had ever happened in Jewish culture. They had no other benchmarks of persecution against which to judge. Perhaps, too, God, in His wisdom and mercy, intentionally withheld the final judgment until some later time. Conditions may have changed to a degree He thought it best to delay the end times. Answers to this speculation will only be revealed to us when we are in glory together.

They went out from us, but they were not of us; for if they had been of us, they would have continued with us; but they went out that they might be made manifest, that none of them were of us.

1st John 2:19

"Went out from us," that is, separated from the fellowship doctrinally. Doubtless then, as now, the deniers of the Son still called themselves Christians. Such departures from the faith were not new.

"Corrupt men have gone out from among you and enticed the inhabitants of their city, saying, "Let us go and serve other gods" "- which you have not known -

"then you shall inquire, search out, and ask diligently. And if it is indeed true and certain that such an abomination was committed among you,

"you shall surely strike the inhabitants of that city with the edge of the sword-utterly destroying it, all that is in it and its livestock, with the edge of the sword.

Deuteronomy 13:13–15

What is distinctive about these defectors is Satan's intention to use them to fragment and weaken the church.

> *This you know, that all those in Asia have turned away from me, among whom are Phygellus and Hermogenes.*
>
> **2nd Timothy 1:15**

> *For there must also be factions among you, that those who are approved may be recognized among you.*
>
> *1ˢᵗ* **Corinthians 11:19**

Writing to the much troubled congregation at Corinth, Paul admits there were splinter groups within the church, but says those true to the faith were easily identified. His worry was the potentially alluring away by false doctrine so similar to the truth that believers could become easily confused. Paul seemed to be particularly hounded by such troublemakers but he recognized that even so the Word of God was being spread in some form. In Philippians he praises the fact there are others preaching Christ while he is imprisoned (Those individuals challenged Paul's leadership, not necessarily the doctrines he preached.)

John's first epistle reinforces Paul's comfort. If one is living a Christian life, saturated with the Holy Spirit, they are easily recognized. This reinforces the concept both men so often repeat: if one is truly saved and has received the Holy Spirit, then one can only live a righteous life. Any behavior not in alignment with Jesus' teachings signifies a life not truly committed to godliness.

The departure from the fellowship of those adhering to false teachings will be easily spotted. As an added bonus because of their departure, the church was purged and strengthened. The spiritual pruning made the tender shoot of early Christianity tougher and taller. The early church moved forward much faster without having to drag along those who sought to dilute Jesus' teachings.

> *But you have an anointing from the Holy One, and you know all things.*
>
> *1ˢᵗ* **John 2:20**

As so often is the case John reminds his readers of what they already have. Having committed their lives to Jesus, they have been filled with the Holy Spirit, a holy anointing providing all the knowledge needed to live a Christian life. Kings, prophets, and priests were anointed in token of receiving divine grace. All believers are, in a secondary sense, what Christ was in a primary sense, "the Lord's anointed." Anointing was the inaugural ceremony for priests in which they were covered, head to toe with an unguent, an ointment, usually prepared by the Hebrews from oil and aromatic herbs. John's use of the word confirms the spiritual anointing of believers was complete, touching every fiber of their body and life. It was a confirmation from God of their faith.

John writes "you know all things." The pronoun is inclusive, encompassing those who were actual witnesses to Christ's teaching, and those to whom it has been carried by first century evangelists. The power of the Holy Spirit and the spiritual nature of the scriptures include us today. The power of the saving grace of Jesus extends through the ages.

Even though there were then (and are today) those misleading and deceiving Jesus' followers, we've been blessed and are protected by God and His Holy Spirit. We have the knowledge in our hearts and confirmed by the Spirit; we know the truth; we _are_ the truth. The defense is available; it is our willful decision to use it or not.

In Case You've Forgotten – 1st John 2:21-29

I have not written to you because you do not know the truth, but because you know it, and that no lie is of the truth.

1ˢᵗ John 2:21

J ohn, the careful teacher, repeats once more a reason for his having put this epistle together. The purpose of the letter was not to teach new things. The chaotic and perilous times made it necessary to reiterate the essential themes of Christianity. This letter was to be a refresher course for believers. It serves today as a basic inventory against which we all need to measure ourselves.

John picks up his megaphone and starts once more to preach against those who seek to deceive others and misrepresent the faith.

Who is a liar but he who denies that Jesus is the Christ?
he is antichrist who denies the Father and the Son.

1ˢᵗ John 2:22

The word he uses for *liar* describes one who breaks faith, a false and faithless man. It fits in with his appraisal of the antichrist. Now John adds that not only does this evil one deny Jesus, but also refuses to acknowledge God! Rejection of the deity of the Son must also reject the authority and existence of the Father. Taking such a position brings into doubt the entire purpose of creation. It threatens to unsettle every belief system in existence. Every foundational concept of religion is called into question.

But if we embrace Jesus as LORD, then we also accept His relationship to God. We fully recognize Him as Creator and author of everything. It follows that we recognize Christ as his Son, and the atoning death He suffered as sacrifice for our sinfulness.

This is the second of six times John uses his exclusive term to describe this emissary of the devil who seeks to destroy the church.

Whoever denies the Son does not have the Father either; he who acknowledges the Son has the Father also.

Therefore let that abide in you which you heard from the beginning. If what you heard from the beginning abides in you, you also will abide in the Son and in the Father.

1ˢᵗ John 2:23–24

John restates the premise that denial of one of the Trinity means denial of the other two parts, but he offers reassurance that acknowledgment of any part of the Trinity means acceptance of all three. He adds further comfort that if believers have kept these concepts in their hearts and truly believe them, then their defense and protection by Christ and the LORD is assured. John is very determined to declare to his "little children" that their faithfulness is rewarded. The blessing of the fellowship with Jesus and other followers is, to John, the ultimate solace in a troubled world.

And this is the promise that he has promised us-eternal life.

1ˢᵗ John 2:25

Here it is again – the straight forward, simple truth of what faith in Jesus offers. It is the reward for all the patience, diligence and service in this frustratingly corrupt existence., We are granted eternal life in heaven. But one has to take the entire passage into context to understand this promise is only fulfilled if we accept the divine relationship between the Father and the Son.

"And as Moses lifted up the serpent in the wilderness, even so must the Son of Man be lifted up,

"that whoever believes in Him should not perish but have eternal life.

> *"For God so loved the world that he gave His only begotten Son, that whoever believes in Him should not perish but have everlasting life.*
>
> ***John 3:14–16***

Go back to John's familiar essential statement of the gospel. He doesn't repeat it in this epistle even though it is a cornerstone of the faith, but one must accept the sacrificial gift of Christ to be granted the gift of salvation. Christ made this statement in private to Nicodemus in their nighttime conversation.

Jesus repeats this promise later in his public ministry.

> *"And this is the will of Him who sent Me, that everyone who sees the Son and believes in Him may have everlasting life; and I will raise him up at the last day."*
>
> ***John 6:40***

Later Our Savior prays that this gift will be accepted by those who hear His teaching:

> *Jesus spoke these words, lifted up His eyes to heaven, and said: "Father, the hour has come. Glorify Your Son, that Your Son also may glorify You,*
>
> *"as You have given Him authority over all flesh, that he should give eternal life to as many as You have given Him.*
>
> *"And this is eternal life, that they may know You, the only true God, and Jesus Christ whom You have sent.*
>
> ***John 17:1–3***

In verse 3 Jesus defines for us "eternal life:" as knowing God and his Son. In this context the word "know" is to learn, get a knowledge of, perceive, feel; to become acquainted with, This means an intellectual acceptance and acknowledgment of God's existence and the purpose of His Son. It is more than a causal acceptance of a dogma but a steadfast adherence to its veracity, the willingness to defend it from all assaults, even to the point of death and sacrifice. It is ___not___ a wise man glorying in his own wisdom, a mighty man reassured by his own strength, a rich man comforted by his own wealth. It is one who understands God's will, accepts it, and seeks to glorify the LORD in everything they do.

> *Thus says the Lord: "Let not the wise man glory in his wisdom, Let not the mighty man glory in his might, Nor let the rich man glory in his riches;*
>
> *But let him who glories glory in this, That he understands and knows Me, That I am the Lord, exercising loving-kindness, judgment, and righteousness in the earth. For in these I delight," says the Lord.*

> ***Jeremiah 9:23–24***

Jesus accurately reflects God's words because Christ <u>*is*</u> the Holy Spirit, the same spirit given to all believers on an "all or nothing" basis. There are no half-measures in its granting.

In summing up verses 1st John 2:23-25, we can say the specific heresy against which John preaches is a denial of the incarnation of God in Christ which provided for the total attainment of a personal relationship with Christ and God.

> *These things I have written to you concerning those who try to deceive you.*

> ***1st John 2:26***

John concludes his warning with a reiteration of his purpose in writing, "to warn."

> *But the anointing which you have received from Him abides in you, and you do not need that anyone teach you; but as the same anointing teaches you concerning all things, and is true, and is not a lie, and just as it has taught you, you will abide in Him.*

> ***1st John 2:27***

John reassures his readers (going on the assumption that all his readers are believers) if they have received the teaching and **are** believers, then the Spirit and His teaching is already in them; they are not threatened by the heresies which are out there. Their protection and defense is assured.

The anointing of which he speaks is, of course, the gift of the Holy Spirit. This gift to us is Jesus' personal request on our behalf of the Father. Because His presence confirms our membership in the Family of God, one can consider the Holy Spirit as our "spiritual circumcision." Paul does in fact make this comparison many times. It is the hard, physical and outward sign of our devotion to Jesus as Savior.

"Human teaching" is necessary to get us started in our relationship with God; the LORD gives to many this gift. It is the Holy Spirit who takes what we have seen, read and felt, then "burns" it into our hearts. Human thought works with the Spirit. One of John's purposes in writing is to help believers learn to discern between those who are truly conduits of Godly principles and those used by Satan to confuse and disrupt fellowship. He also affirms that those who are tested and proved to be valid communicators should be honored and respected, but cautions that it is the *Spirit* who teaches what is right, *not* people. John is not saying we don't need teachers; what he is saying is that if there is a conflict between what is being taught and what the Holy Spirit tells *us*, our allegiance should be with the Spirit. With this understanding, the apostle's warnings about the antichrist are clearer and more precise.

> *And now, little children, abide in Him, that when he appears, we may have confidence and not be ashamed before Him at His coming.*

> *1st John 2:28*

John returns (as he so often does in his writings) to the one valid solution to proper living – live in fellowship with Jesus (and thus with others) so that when He returns we will possess two things: we will have courage enough to believe in Christ, and we will not be fearful because of any personal shame when we are face-to-face with Jesus.

The "coming" was the official, formal phrase used at that time to describe the arrival of a high representative. It is used 18 times in the New Testament, referring to the appearance of the incarnate Son of God. The use of the phrase would instantly convey to the average person the significance of the event, and also the power and authority involved in the event. The phrase also connotes the establishment of a permanent, personal relationship.

John's reassurance to his "little children" is that if they have been cautious, avoided the lure of the false teachers he has identified, then there should be nothing for them to fear at the return of Christ for they will surely receive from Him their just rewards.

> *If you know that he is righteous, you know that everyone who practices righteousness is born of Him.*
>
> *1ˢᵗ John 2:29*

John closes his second chapter with a standard for righteousness. Recognizing the fruits of the Spirit in Christ is easy, and it should be the measuring stick by which we recognize fellow believers. The key element of this verse is the "practices" requirement. John uses a word that encompasses continual, constant performance. That is the key to distinguishing believers from pretenders. As we've noted many time before in these first two chapters, it is consistency in behavior that is the clue to one's heart. John winds up this second chapter with a reminder of that.

This is not said as if there were any doubt but to call attention to a well-known truth. Everyone with any knowledge of God should have the conviction that He is a righteous Being. But, if this be so, John says, only those who are truly righteous can regard themselves as begotten of Him.

The Greek phrase for "*you know*" will bear both constructions, and either would make good sense. Assuming that God is righteous, it would be proper to state, as in the text, that only those who are righteous can be regarded as begotten of Him; or, assuming this to be true, it was proper to exhort them to be righteous, as the text is rendered in the margin notes. Whichever interpretation is adopted, the great truth is taught, that only those who are truly righteous can regard themselves as the children of God.

Everyone that does righteousness is born of Him, or rather, is begotten of Him; they are truly a child of God. This truth is taught throughout the Bible, and is worthy of being often repeated. No one who is not a righteous man can have any other well-founded pretensions. It is not difficult to determine whether we are the children of God.

If we are unjust, false, dishonest, we cannot be His children.

If we are indulging in any known sin, we cannot be.

If we are not truly righteous, all visions, all zeal and ardor, though in the cause of religion, all we pride ourselves in, even being fervent in prayer or eloquent in preaching, is in vain.

If we are righteous, in the true and proper sense, doing what is right toward God and toward people, to ourselves, to our families, to our neighbors, to the world at large, to the Savior who died for us, then we are true Christians. Then, no matter how soon He may appear, or how solemn and overwhelming the scenes that shall close the world, we shall not be ashamed or confounded, for we shall hail Him as our Savior, and rejoice that the time has come that we may go and dwell with Him forever.

A Child's Life – 1st John 3:1-2

John's gospel is perhaps the most symbol-filled of the four yet his epistles are informal, personal, revealing a deep affection for his audience. His fatherly concern springs from the reverence shown to him. Remember that at the time of the distribution of the letters, he was the only survivor of the original disciples. Only Paul may have been as well-known by more believers. He seems to have accepted the paternal authority thrust upon him willingly, and sought, through his persuasive style to lead his beloved "little children" down the correct path.

As we've seen in Chapter Two, he was fighting a massive heresy in the church. The separation of the teachers from the church would, by the Second Century, spring into the full-blown sect of Gnosticism, teaching that matter is essentially evil, and spirit is essentially good. Their refusal to accept the concept of a spiritual God inhabiting a material body led to their denial of Jesus' deity, and thus a denial of the resurrection. They preached the body Christ inhabited could not have been real, but was merely "apparent."

Thus far John has written a defense of the Incarnation in Chapter One and a description and standard for the life of righteousness in Chapter Two. Chapter Three begins his detailing the life of the children of God.

> *Behold what manner of love the Father has bestowed on us, that we should be called children of God! Therefore the world does not know us, because it did not know Him.*

> *1ˢᵗ John 3:1*

Envision Charles Wesley snatching up his quill when he came to this passage and out flowed "*AMAZING LOVE.*" Believers are "children of God," __the__ God, simply because we have accepted Jesus as our savior and acknowledged His death for our sins and His resurrection as proof of His deity

The plural, "children of God," is sometimes used to denote the pious descendants of Seth. In other usages, the phrase is interpreted to mean the angels. Hosea uses the phrase to designate the gracious relation in which men stand to God. But John applies it to those of his flock. In his Gospel, John conveys the same concept:

> *[...]he would gather together in one the children of God who were scattered abroad.*

> *John 11:52*

The adopted are to be gathered together, in one place at one time, by Christ. As John viewed the world around him, he could see the first stirrings of this in-gathering.

The problem was, if one even considered it a problem, the world, not having eyes that could perceive the nature of Jesus, did not recognize believers as anything special or unique. They were "different" because they followed different standards but the stubborn hearts on the outside of the church could not accept their distinctiveness as anything good.

> *Beloved, now we are children of God; and it has not yet been revealed what we shall be, but we know that when he is revealed, we shall be like Him, for we shall see Him as he is.*

> *1st John 3:2*

John reassures his readers they *are* children, but wonders exactly what the fully glorified form of that existence will be. This ties together with verse 1 in that the existence John speaks of is in the future, at the time of Christ's fully established kingdom.

> *For you did not receive the spirit of bondage again to fear, but you received the Spirit of adoption by whom we cry out, "Abba, Father."*

> *The Spirit Himself bears witness with our spirit that we are children of God,*

> *and if children, then heirs-heirs of God and joint heirs*
> *with Christ, if indeed we suffer with Him, that we may*
> *also be glorified together.*
>
> **Romans 8:15–17**

Paul agrees that believers have been given the special gift of adoption as direct descendants of God, *and* the Holy Spirit. In Paul's conceptualization, the Holy Spirit is confirmation of our membership in God's household.

> *For I consider that the sufferings of this present time*
> *are not worthy to be compared with the glory which*
> *shall be revealed in us.*
>
> *For the earnest expectation of the creation eagerly*
> *waits for the revealing of the sons of God.*
>
> **Romans 8:18–19**

> *Not only that, but we also who have the first fruits of*
> *the Spirit, even we ourselves groan within ourselves,*
> *eagerly waiting for the adoption, the redemption of our*
> *body.*
>
> **Romans 8:23**

Paul continues that one of the graces bestowed on members of God's family is coming glorification, a "reward" (so to speak) for having endured the trials of our earthly life. He amplifies his concept of the future kingdom to say that not only will we humans revel in it, but "all creation" is anticipating it and will join in the celebration of its culmination.

Paul does step out a little more boldly in trying to imagine our future form than John. He says we shall be more like Christ.

> *For whom he foreknew, he also predestined to be*
> *conformed to the image of His Son, that he might be the*
> *firstborn among many brethren.*
>
> **Romans 8:29**

> *But we all, with unveiled face, beholding as in a mirror*
> *the glory of the Lord, are being transformed into the*

same image from glory to glory, just as by the Spirit of the Lord.

2ⁿᵈ *Corinthians 3:18*

We are being conformed to the image of the Son of God, and transformed into the glory of the LORD.

Not a bad metamorphosis.

Hope Ahead – 1st John 3:3-7

J ohn continues, speaking about the "hope" for those who are not yet believers, what they might attain.

> *And everyone who has this hope in Him purifies himself, just as he is pure.*
>
> *1st John 3:3*

The word John uses for "purifying" refers to being ceremonially clean, and morally spotless. This provides reassurance of the forgiveness of sins which means the gift of eternal life.

The word he uses for "pure" connotes exciting reverence, venerable, sacred, and being free from carnality, living in a chaste, modest, faultless, and immaculate manner. This aligns with the promise of total forgiveness by Jesus to those who follow Him, and to Isaiah's promise:

> *"Come now, and let us reason together," Says the Lord, "Though your sins are like scarlet, They shall be as white as snow; Though they are red like crimson, They shall be as wool.*
>
> *Isaiah 1:18*

The basic impetus for becoming a Christian is the promise of being thus transformed with the firm assurance of forgiveness and everlasting life. This is motivation enough for a righteous life. Approval like that fulfills that basic human need for acceptance and belonging.

> *Whoever commits sin also commits lawlessness, and sin is lawlessness.*
>
> *1st John 3:4*

John reverts back to the subject of sin and introduces a syllogism securely equating sinfulness with violation of the Mosaic Law. Sin is "any want of conformity unto or transgression of the law of God" and in the inward state and habit of the soul, as well as in the outward conduct of the life, whether by omission or commission. It is not a mere violation of the law of our constitution, nor of the system of things, but an offense against the personal lawgiver and moral governor, God in Christ, who vindicates His law with penalties. Sinners are always conscious that sin is intrinsically vile and polluting, and that it justly deserves punishment by calling down the righteous wrath of God; the problem is they just don't care. True sin is not accidental or unintentional; it is deliberate, though not always pre-meditated. That is what makes sinful living so distasteful to God. The perpetrator knows what they are doing and makes the conscious decision to stray from the path of righteousness.

Paul's masterful treatise on the essentials of Christian faith is Romans. In chapter 4, he explains the nature of the Law of Moses and bluntly says it is the source of a great deal of suffering

> *because the law brings about wrath; for where there is no law there is no transgression.*
>
> *Romans 4:15*

Paul says that the Law defines "sin" as violations of standards, codes and procedures. It has the consequence of divine wrath for failure to meet its requirements. The wrath is not meant as a punishment for those who diligently and honestly try to follow the Law's requirements, but as a means of keeping the kingdom purified so those unworthy are denied entrance and put aside. The integrity of the Kingdom is maintained because sinfulness is not acceptable within it.

Paul establishes our culpability when he writes

> *Therefore by the deeds of the law no flesh will be justified in His sight, for by the law is the knowledge of sin.*
>
> *Romans 3:20*

If one knows there is a law, Paul reasons, then one knows what is sinful. If one knows what is sinful, then failure to steer clear of it requires eternal punishment. The law sets the standards by which we are to be judged. If we know the standards, then we also know what is not acceptable. Having that knowledge then means we can rightly be punished when we fail to keep the law *because we knew what was right and didn't do it,*

This has been a long way around to re-state the obvious: sinfulness and breaking the Mosaic Law ("lawlessness") are the same; both will keep you from entering into heaven.

> *And you know that he was manifested to take away our sins, and in Him there is no sin.*
>
> *1ˢᵗ John 3:5*

Christ came to grant us forgiveness from failing to adhere to the Law. His sacrifice was an acceptable substitute for us because he was sinless and blameless. John the Baptist said in John 1:29 that Jesus was "The Lamb of God who takes away the sin of the world!" He was the ultimate sacrifice, able to atone for all the wickedness of all humanity.

One of the goals of His ministry was "For he made Him who knew no sin to be sin for us, that we might become the righteousness of God in Him." (2ⁿᵈ Corinthians 5:21). This provides righteous covering for those who were sinful by exchanging His sinless life for ours. He suffered the punishment we should have received in order to take away the guilt of our lives.

John's comments elsewhere in his first letter make it very clear he is not referring to continual, habitual, unrepentant, sinful living. Such a person is not a believer and doesn't qualify for the grace of Jesus. Followers of Christ from then until now know living a life in defiance of His grace is not acceptable; it is living in darkness, which is not where the followers of Jesus live. John says it again here:

> *Whoever abides in Him does not sin. Whoever sins has neither seen Him nor known Him.*
>
> *1ˢᵗ John 3:6*

Renouncing and abandoning a sinful lifestyle is the surest measure of one's devotion and acceptance of the Savior. The word used for "sees" is related to "blindness" (a condition which disqualified one for Old Testament priestly service). John, though, is speaking of spiritual blindness, as exhibited by Pharaoh to Moses –

> *And Pharaoh said, "Who is the Lord, that I should obey His voice to let Israel go? I do not know the Lord, nor will I let Israel go."*
>
> ***Exodus 5:2***

And Samson, blinded by his lust for Delilah, also was afflicted with it.

> *And she said, "The Philistines are upon you, Samson!" So he awoke from his sleep, and said, "I will go out as before, at other times, and shake myself free!" But he did not know that the Lord had departed from him.*
>
> ***Judges 16:20***
>
> *The fool has said in his heart, "There is no God." They are corrupt, They have done abominable works, There is none who does good.*
>
> ***Psalms 14:1***

As the end of the historical Israel drew near, Jeremiah reminded the people of how spiritually blind they were.

> *The priests did not say, "Where is the Lord?" And those who handle the law did not know Me; The rulers also transgressed against Me; The prophets prophesied by Baal, And walked after things that do not profit.*
>
> ***Jeremiah 2:8***

So this spiritual blindness was not new one to the Jews of Jesus' day. John cites it as a major danger in the young church. That self-possessed, self-assurance, that deceiving attitude of self-righteousness coming from an internal evaluation is so often wrong. We can find fault in others and relish in finger pointing but fail miserably in acknowledging the same faults in ourselves. To non-believers, this hypocrisy is the major excuse for rejecting Jesus. This very real malfunction of the church threatens its very survival.

This is such a significant issue to John he continues to draw contrasts between the valid life and the vapid life.

> *Little children, let no one deceive you. he who practices righteousness is righteous, just as he is righteous.*

> *Ist John 3:7*

John is using a word for *"righteousness"* that in a broad sense means a state of being acceptable to God. In ordinary experience it is integrity, virtue, purity of life, rightness, correctness of thinking feeling, and acting. In a narrower sense, it is the justice applied to each one of us as recompense for the nature of our living. It is giving everyone what they are due. Paul gives an extended description of Abraham who had attained "righteousness."

> *For what does the Scripture say? "Abraham believed God, and it was accounted to him for righteousness." [...]*

> *But to him who does not work but believes on Him who justifies the ungodly, his faith is accounted for righteousness, [...]*

> *Does this blessedness then come upon the circumcised only, or upon the uncircumcised also? For we say that faith was accounted to Abraham for righteousness.[...]*

> *And he received the sign of circumcision, a seal of the righteousness of the faith which he had while still uncircumcised, that he might be the father of all those who believe, though they are uncircumcised, that righteousness might be imputed to them also, [...]*

> *he did not waver at the promise of God through unbelief, but was strengthened in faith, giving glory to God, [...].*

> *And therefore "it was accounted to him for righteousness."[...]*

> *but also for us. It shall be imputed to us who believe in Him who raised up Jesus our Lord from the dead,*

> **Romans 4:3, 5, 9, 11, 13, 20, 22, 24** [10]

At this point in history, John was well aware of the Hebrews passage and Paul's verses. All he had to do was to mention the magic word "righteousness" and instantly the image would spring into the mind of believers. It resonated with their Jewish roots and it carried them forward with Christ's reassurance of salvation.

The Main Event – 1st John 3:8-12

S atan, or the Devil, or whatever name you apply to him, is real. I recently was reading a book on prophecy by a female writer claiming to be an evangelical Christian. When she made the statement she did not believe in an actual Satan, that sinfulness and evil were merely states of mind, I put the book aside. How can anyone deny such? Jesus Himself refers to Satan as an existing personage (or angelness, I imagine). And one then drops back to C.S. Lewis' argument that what Christ says must be true, or he was a raving lunatic. One cannot pick and choose which of Christ's words are true. If you accept Him as Lord, then you have to accept every and each word as true; there is no falseness in Him, which is what John has been drumming into us so far in this first epistle.

Now John turns to another aspect and purpose of Christ's ministry, the conquest of Satan.

> *he who sins is of the devil, for the devil has sinned from the beginning. For this purpose the Son of God was manifested, that he might destroy the works of the devil.*
>
> *1ˢᵗ John 3:8*

John again draws on the knowledge base of his "little children," for they all knew of Satan's origin. John flatly states one purpose of Christ's incarnation was to defeat the Evil One and his works. Satan has been active from the beginning of time but Jesus was revealed to unmask the wickedness of Satan. An important distinction needs to be made: Christ's purpose in His first coming was to destroy the *works* of the Devil; the total obliteration of the person Satan is not to take place until the Second Coming and the great apocalyptic battle of Armageddon.

> *"The field is the world, the good seeds are the sons of
> the kingdom, but the tares are the sons of the wicked
> one.*
>
> *Matthew 13:38*

The "tares" of wheat are the useless kernel-like nodules that can be
mistaken for the valuable grain. They are separated from the good
kernels through a process of being tossed in a breeze; being lighter,
they are blown away and discarded. The heavier, useful grains drop
back into the winnowing basket. This process is so descriptive of the
manner in which God deals with His people, and those who claim to
be believers. They are "tossed" and have to endure winds of change
and adversity, but they land safely back in the "basket" of the LORD.

> *"And this gospel of the kingdom will be preached in all
> the world as a witness to all the nations, and then the
> end will come.*
>
> *Matthew 24:14*

Christ tells his disciples what will be done with His message of
redemption and His castigation of the works and world of the Devil.
But, note the construction of the sentence is such that the preaching
and witnessing must be done *"and then"* the end will come. Not until
every opportunity has been exhausted to spread the gospel will the
Second Coming begin. This should be of some comfort, especially to
those who believe and fear the tribulation is just around the corner.
Other gospel accounts confirm this.

> *And he said to them, "Go into <u>all the world</u> and preach
> the gospel to every creature.*
>
> *Mark 16:15 [emphasis added]*

> *And he said to them, "Go into all the world and preach
> the gospel to every creature.*
>
> *Luke 24:47*

The identical wording of the Mark and Luke passages is strong
evidence of some central source for Christ's sermons and instructions

to his disciples, even though the authors (Mark and Like) were years apart and different backgrounds – a confirmation of the spiritual and supernatural guidance of the Holy Spirit in the writing of the New Testament.

The Apostle Paul quotes an Old Testament source stating that God's message of righteousness has already been spread through the world, not just to believers (read *Jews*).

> *But I say, have they not heard? Yes indeed: "Their sound has gone out to all the earth, And their words to the ends of the world."*
>
> **Romans 10:18**
>
> *which has come to you, as it has also in all the world, and is bringing forth fruit, as it is also among you since the day you heard and knew the grace of God in truth;*
>
> **Colossians 1:6**

Scholars of the day knew the figure of whom Christ spoke. He had been identified by Moses in his Old Testament writing of Geneses:

> *"And I will put enmity Between you and the woman, And between your seed and her Seed; he shall bruise your head, And you shall bruise His heel."*
>
> **Genesis 3:15**

This "seed" is the family of Satan, his followers and those of his kingdom of evil darkness. It is they who fight so persistently and with such stealth against God's righteous people.

All this gets wrapped together in John's gospel:

> *"You are of your father the devil, and the desires of your father you want to do. he was a murderer from the beginning, and does not stand in the truth, because there is no truth in him. When he speaks a lie, he speaks from his own resources, for he is a liar and the father of it.*
>
> **John 8:44**

Jesus plainly says those who do not love Him are children of Satan, and are part of Satan's domain. His focus is on the deceitfulness of Satan which ties neatly to the pretense of being righteous.

The other major New Testament writer, Luke, also subscribes so the concept Satan and the world being deceitful and undesirable.

> *and* [Paul] *said, "O full of all deceit and all fraud, you*[Elymas, the sorcerer] *son of the devil, you enemy of all righteousness, will you not cease perverting the straight ways of the Lord?*
>
> *"And now, indeed, the hand of the Lord is upon you, and you shall be blind, not seeing the sun for a time." And immediately a dark mist fell on him, and he went around seeking someone to lead him by the hand.*
>
> *Acts 13:10–11*

This report of Paul's confrontation with someone seeking to undermine the believers' work by objecting to Paul's strong condemnation of Elymas, reaffirms the judgment. And it buttresses Christ's direction to His followers to resist Satan.

Jesus sent his disciples out on a missionary journey on their own. They came back and reported to Him how it went. Luke, the beloved physician gospel writer, records His reaction and response.

> *And he said to them, "I saw Satan fall like lightning from heaven.*
>
> *"Behold, I give you the authority to trample on serpents and scorpions, and over all the power of the enemy, and nothing shall by any means hurt you.*
>
> *"Nevertheless do not rejoice in this, that the spirits are subject to you, but rather rejoice because your names are written in heaven."*
>
> *In that hour Jesus rejoiced in the Spirit and said, "I thank You, Father, Lord of heaven and earth, that You have hidden these things from the wise and prudent and*

revealed them to babes. Even so, Father, for so it seemed good in Your sight.

"All things have been delivered to Me by My Father, and no one knows who the Son is except the Father, and who the Father is except the Son, and the one to whom the Son wills to reveal Him."

Then he turned to His disciples and said privately, "Blessed are the eyes which see the things you see;

"for I tell you that many prophets and kings have desired to see what you see, and have not seen it, and to hear what you hear, and have not heard it."

Luke 10:18-24

Jesus summed up the ultimate disposition of Satan to His disciples, but cautioned the power they had, and that we have, needs to be exercised with the understanding of its responsibility. And He cautioned that the world, the unsaved, would never appreciate their work and could not acknowledge their authority.

Whoever has been born of God does not sin, for His seed remains in him; and he cannot sin, because he has been born of God.

1ˢᵗ John 3:9

This circles back to John's assertion that anyone who is a believer cannot "accidentally" sin since the nature that is in a believer is the nature of God, and God is sinless. It is a reassurance designed to comfort and strengthen Christians, not to worry them. A believer's basic character is Christ-like, and when they stumble, forgiveness and restoration is available.

All things were made through Him, and without Him nothing was made that was made.

John 1:3

Jesus clarifies this statement–

> *Jesus answered and said to him, "Most assuredly, I say to you, unless one is born again, he cannot see the kingdom of God."*

John 3:3

Jesus' other favorite apostle, Peter, confirms this by writing

> *Since you have purified your souls in obeying the truth through the Spirit in sincere love of the brethren, love one another fervently with a pure heart,*
>
> *having been born again, not of corruptible seed but incorruptible, through the word of God which lives and abides forever,*
>
> *because "All flesh is as grass, And all the glory of man as the flower of the grass. The grass withers, And its flower falls away,"*

1st Peter 1:22–24

The potential nature of God placed within us in our creation on our conversion is refreshed when we are born again. Though we live in a fallen world, the essence of our creation is to be "like God" not like Satan. We are all sinners and fall short of the glory of God because of Adam's fall, and our need for a savior is real. The blessing is that it only takes making that step of faith in acceptance of Christ as our Savior to reconstitute the godly nature in us. Like astronauts who squirt a little water into a sealed plastic bag and get in return a nutritious meal, a spritz of Jesus in our soul restores our heaven-bound character.

> *Now to Him who is able to keep you from stumbling, And to present you faultless Before the presence of His glory with exceeding joy,*

Jude 24

Those who challenge the faith point out that it is impossible to live a "sinless" life. That is true; one cannot help but commit acts which do not meet the LORD's standards. But that is not what John and Jesus are talking about. The criterion is "continual sinning." John has already explained to his little children that those who live a life of sin, sinning every day and in every way, are not living a believer's life. Everyone stumbles, all the time. But it is the getting up after falling down that makes the difference. It is the effort one makes towards restoration that is the measure of dedication. The truthfulness of one's faith is seen by the behavior after the sin, the *life* that is lived as a whole, not judged by the individual breakdowns.

> *In this the children of God and the children of the devil are manifest: Whoever does not practice righteousness is not of God, nor is he who does not love his brother.*

> *1ˢᵗ John 3:10*

John begins another repetition of a major contrast – "the children of God" and "the children of the devil." The point is simple enough, but a literal translation of the verse reads

> *In this manifest are the children of God, and the children of the devil; every one who is not doing righteousness, is not of God, and he who is not loving his brother,*

> *1 John 3:10*

A "child *of God*" practices righteousness and loves fellow believers. Those "not *of God*" do not practice righteousness and do not love others. "*Practicing*" our faith means to produce, to bring about, to cause to be, and to bear (as a crop) a result or action. "Practicing righteousness" is not simply following rules; it is *work*, diligence and concentrated effort. "Righteousness" here means the virtuous life which is the result of salvation through Christ. The righteous man under law became righteous by doing righteously; under grace he does righteously because he has been made righteous.

even the righteousness of God, through faith in Jesus Christ, to all and on all who believe. For there is no difference;

Romans 3:22

This Pauline reference circles us back to the next passage in 1ˢᵗ John:

For this is the message that you heard from the beginning, that we should love one another,

1ˢᵗ John 3:11

This repetition of a foundational gospel element is intentional, as we've seen. John views it as an absolute necessity for believers to grasp, understand and live as Christ directed.

"A new commandment I give to you, that you love one another; as I have loved you, that you also love one another.

"By this all will know that you are My disciples, if you have love for one another."

John 13:34-35

Which is in itself a repetition of that Old Testament commandment

"You shall not take vengeance, nor bear any grudge against the children of your people, but you shall love your neighbor as yourself: I am the Lord.

Leviticus 19:18

the instruction given by God to the Hebrews as they entered into the Promised Land of Canaan. As noted in Chapter One, this commandment is considered by Christ to be *the* foundational, fundamental law.

not as Cain who was of the wicked one and murdered his brother. And why did he murder him? Because his [Cain's]works were evil and his brother"s righteous.

1ˢᵗ John 3:12

Many studies have been written on what it was that displeased the LORD with Cain's sacrifice. The best explanation I have found is that Cain was guilty of a "poor quality of worship." Something in his attitude about making the offering – perhaps frustration at having to do so in the first place (like many men today who feel dragged to church by wives and children), a regret that he had to give up a portion of what he had worked hard to produce, a feeling of not being able to measure up to his older brother – spoke to God, who suggested Cain re-evaluate his act of sacrifice. As so often is the case, Cain lashed out at the individual physically nearest him at the time, blaming Abel for this heavenly rebuke. His commission of murder was out of anger, frustration and envy. Today's criminal defense attorneys would have cited "temporary insanity" or "post-harvest stress syndrome" as explanations. John attributes the evil act to Cain's resentment of his brother's success. John says this is how a lack of love for another leads to a sinful attitude and a sinful life. John's example reflects the danger one faces when there is a lack of love and respect for others. Cain should have been happy his brother's sacrifice was sufficient, and anxious to correct his shortcomings. Instead, John says, he hated his brother and killed him.

Cain (whose name means "acquisition') is a type of the mere man of the earth. His religion was destitute of any adequate sense of sin, or need of atonement. Seemingly, despite the teaching of his father Adam, he worshiped in self-will and was angry with God. What was the source of his anger? It could have been that he had to *work* to live; being a farmer is no easy task. His brother Abel seemed to survive by the seemingly easy life of a hunter.

Cain refused to bring a sin offering. Since the formal sacrificial system had not established, Adam's instructions may have been a little vague but it most certainly would have included guidance on the offering of an animal to the LORD as an offering. Cain disregarded that teaching.

All these frustrations boiled over in Cain and he murdered his brother then compounds his heinous act by lying to God . God's judgment forces him to become a vagabond but in the midst of his punishment Cain is, nevertheless, the object of the divine solicitude in that the mark placed on him by God prevents him from dying violently like his brother.

Abel ('exhalation," or, "that which ascends') is a type of the spiritual man. His sacrifice, in which atoning blood was shed was therefore at once his confession of sin and the expression of his faith in the interposition of a substitute.

Taught by their father, the two brothers were trained in the duty of worshiping God. "And in process of time', i.e., on the Sabbath, each of them offered up to God of the first-fruits of his labors. Cain, as a husbandman, offered the fruits of the field; Abel, as a shepherd, of the firstlings of his flock. "The Lord had respect unto Abel and his offering; but unto Cain and his offering he had not respect" because of this Cain was angry with his brother, and formed the design of putting him to death; a design which he at length found an opportunity of carrying into effect.

Why have we dived back to the beginning of the scriptures to this story? Because John made the reference to Cain's sinfulness and one must fully comprehend what that was to grasp the significance of John's teaching.

Being a Child of God -1st John 3:13-17

Do not marvel, my brethren, if the world hates you.

We know that we have passed from death to life, because we love the brethren. he who does not love his brother abides in death.

Whoever hates his brother is a murderer, and you know that no murderer has eternal life abiding in him.

By this we know love, because he laid down His life for us. And we also ought to lay down our lives for the brethren.

But whoever has this world's goods, and sees his brother in need, and shuts up his heart from him, how does the love of God abide in him?

1ˢᵗ John 3:13–17

T his is one of the rare cases in this study where an entire block of scripture is explained as a whole than as each individual verse. The concepts pile up on each other and tumble together and are much easier to grasp when taken in full. Each is such an integral part of the succeeding point isolating them and analysis is more difficult.

John starts out by repeating that those who do not accept Christ do not love God (acceptance = love) and their allegiance is to the world. The world opposes Christ as a natural consequence of its fallen-ness; it opposes Jesus' teaching and His followers. This shouldn't come as any great surprise. We see the evilness of the world all around; why should it want to change when its way seems to work so well?

The greatest value of our faith is that it spares us eternal separation from God and transforms us with the gift of eternal life. And the criterion by which we are measured is our love for others, not only those who believe as we do, but those who do not. It is loving our enemy that truly reflects our Christ-likeness. Harboring hatred for someone usually means putting no credence in our faith system; we then perpetuate the very attitude we hope to overcome. If that reactive attitude is not changed, those refusing to accept God's grace face eternal damnation and separation. In effect, we have committed murder against them, condemning them to hell by not sharing Jesus' love with them.

We've defined "love" in this book but perhaps it would be beneficial to define what we mean by "hate" because many people would deny hating anyone. We must be clear as to what "hate" encompasses. *To hate* is to have malicious feelings towards others, to intentionally detest another, to fuel acrimony against another. Hate is the absence of desiring only the best for another; one who hates refuses to sacrifice in order to better another. As many different shades of meaning as there are for "love," so are there for "hate.'

This *is* hate:

> *'Most assuredly, I say to you, he who does not enter the sheepfold by the door, but climbs up some other way, the same is a thief and a robber.*

> **John 10:1**

This is *not* hate:

> *'To him the doorkeeper opens, and the sheep hear his voice; and he calls his own sheep by name and leads them out.*

> *'And when he brings out his own sheep, he goes before them; and the sheep follow him, for they know his voice.*

> *'Yet they will by no means follow a stranger, but will flee from him, for they do not know the voice of strangers.'*

> **John 10:2–5**

Jesus illustrates "love" as a total willingness of sacrifice and service. This is the submission of one to the care, nurturing and protection of another, especially one not capable of properly doing it for themselves.

We humans cannot perform the necessary redemption for our sinfulness, but our Lord and Savior can, and does.

The sad element of this passage is John's comment in verse 6.

> *Jesus used this illustration, but they did not understand the things which He spoke to them.*
>
> **John 10:6**

Shepherds were a common part of daily life in 1st Century Israel; though not popular or respected, they were integral to the economy and society. But the people listening to Christ's teaching didn't grasp what He was saying. The hardness of their hearts, so trained by their religious leaders' system of strict adherence to man-made laws, blinded them to the essential principle He was conveying.

The concept of sharing with those less fortunate was a longstanding one. Moses penned the original concept:

> *'If there is among you a poor man of your brethren, within any of the gates in your land which the Lord your God is giving you, you shall not harden your heart nor shut your hand from your poor brother,*
>
> **Deuteronomy 15:7**

Since Christ did as He did for us – dying a painful, humiliating and absolutely unjustified death as a substitute for our sins – then we ought to care for our brothers and sisters. Jesus isn't expecting us all to die for one another, but we should offer up service, care, concern and assistance as a shepherd does for his flock. It is our **_willingness_** to do so that is the measure of our love.

Loving and Living Today
(Part One) - 1st John 3:18-21

The most puzzling and frustrating part of living in today's world is evaluating the lives of others. Many proclaim their faith in God, and their devotion to Christ's teaching. But their behavior is just not matching up with those values. One of my wife's favorite phrases is "They don't get it, they just don't get it,." And a good portion of the population does not "get it." They declare one allegiance, and practice another.

Sacrifice may not always have to be in the submission of a life. We ought to exhibit love by the sharing of material goods as well, and in actions and in encouraging words of hope and instruction. Voluntary love is a confirmation of our faith, the best evidence to the world of Christian life and how it is lived. If we have any doubts about our faith, our "hearts," the Holy Spirit, will point out to us our shortcomings and we can deal with them. If we ask the LORD to forgive us and guide us back on to the path of righteousness, He will, because that is His character. God's love is so great for us He will do anything and everything we ask to keep us in fellowship with Him when we desire it. That desire is not to "claim" or control us, but to provide for us only the very best, the most wonderful future – eternal life and fellowship with Him – for each and every one of us.

But here in verse 18 John is reminding his readers of the responsibility they bear as well. The relationship cannot and will not be unilateral; there must be active attitude, service, witness, and behavior on our side. The beloved apostle is the first to proclaim "We must walk the walk, not just talk the talk." Many pagan religions and false teachers emphasize performance. In fact, much of Christ's displeasure with the scribes and Pharisees was their mindless adherence to the Law and the artificial extensions they had added to God's basic commandments. Much of the religious law imposed by the priests of Christ's time was their own interpretation of what they believed to be augmentations of the commandments given by God to

Moses as recorded in Leviticus and Deuteronomy. What was done was "because it had to be done," not because it was the right and proper thing to do, nor was it what the individual really *wanted* to do. John reiterates that keeping the commandments involves an attitudes as well as an action.

> *My little children, let us not love in word or in tongue,*
> *but in deed and in truth.*
>
> ### 1ˢᵗ *John 3:18*

John breaks out of his exposition with another passionate plea and ringing reassurance. It is almost as though the apostle is desperate for his readers to grasp the concept of living in love and living a life free from deception and falsehood. John knows his readers are familiar with this passage from his own gospel:

> *Pilate therefore said to Him, "Are You a king then?"*
> *Jesus answered, "You say rightly that I am a king. For*
> *this cause I was born, and for this cause I have come*
> *into the world, that I should bear witness to the truth.*
> *Everyone who is of the truth hears My voice.'*
>
> *Pilate said to Him, "What is truth?" And when he had*
> *said this, he went out again to the Jews, and said to*
> *them, "I find no fault in Him at all.*
>
> ### *John 18:37-38*

The guidance of our lives by the Holy Spirit – Christ living within us – is assured but only if we are living "in the truth." Jesus plainly states to the Roman governor the purpose of His coming, aside from the task of salvation (of which Pilate would have no concept), was to permit the world to know and acknowledge divine truth.

> *But the Lord is faithful, who will establish you and*
> *guard you from the evil one.*
>
> *And we have confidence in the Lord concerning you,*
> *both that you do and will do the things we command you.*
>
> ### 2ⁿᵈ *Thessalonians 3:3-4*

Paul writes to believers he has a personal trust that the faithful are living that kind of life. They were expressing their confidence in the LORD with an outward evidence of righteousness and an internal dependence on divine guidance. The benefit of doing so is a reassurance of eternal life. Paul's comments are significant since his context was of the daily struggle against evil and the necessity of using the power of the indwelt Holy Spirit to combat wickedness.

The practical application for us today is that we should take the threat of satanic attacks seriously and we should pray for help and guidance from the LORD. Satan's strategies and tactics are no secret; careful and diligent study of the Bible reveals them, putting us in a better defensive position. Scripture memorization (though not something I am personally able to accomplish) is one way of having God's help in every circumstance. We should keep only friends who are like-minded and who speak the truth in all things. Finally, we must do as Paul has encouraged the Thessalonians, practice what we are taught by spiritual leaders.

> *For if our heart condemns us, God is greater than our heart, and knows all things.*

> *1ˢᵗ John 3:20*

One of the devil's most powerful weapons is creating in us self-doubt, self-criticism. He makes us feel we are unworthy of salvation: "What you have done is so heinous there is no way God will forgive you," Satan whispers in our ears. And yes, though we are unworthy, because of God's great love, we have been forgiven.

Our humanity may tell us we are unacceptable to God when, in fact, we are. But if we are living the right life, God, who knows our hearts even better than we do ourselves, will, through the Holy Spirit, comfort us and reassure us.

> *For I know nothing against myself, yet I am not justified by this; but he who judges me is the Lord.*

> *Therefore judge nothing before the time, until the Lord comes, who will both bring to light the hidden things of*

> *darkness and reveal the counsels of the hearts. Then each one's praise will come from God.*

> *1ˢᵗ Corinthians 4:4–5*

It doesn't matter how we feel about ourselves, if we have asked for forgiveness and the repentance is genuine, then God says we meet His standards. Again, "self" can be the most destructive concept in our lives. Trying to live by "our standards" does no good. It is, or should be, living to God's standards for which we all should strive. Paul reminds us we should not be judging, even judging of ourselves, because the time will come when the LORD will do that. The sentence we deserve will be handed down at the Last Day and Paul has every confidence we believers who struggle to live as the Holy Spirit would have us live, will not be found wanting; we will receive the praise of God.

> *Beloved, if our heart does not condemn us, we have confidence toward God.*

> *1ˢᵗ John 3:21*

Even if we do feel ill–at–ease in approaching the throne of grace, because God knows us and is not put off by what He knows, we should have assurance to come near and worship. We should have no fear of God. At least, not fear in the sense of terror, dread or fright. "Fearing God" properly means to have reverence and to be in awe of Him. He is not holding some celestial fly swatter with which he is going to smack us, especially when we come to Him in sincere repentance.

Our time with Him should begin with praise. Praise is an integral part of worship, and we should daily praise God and give thanks to Him for His grace and forgiveness. There are more things we should thank Him for than we can number; that's why each time we come to God we could spend endless hours reciting the gifts He has given us. When we finally reach that point of confessing our short-comings, it ought to be in the form of thanking Him for granting us grace. Look back at 1ˢᵗ John 2:28; our faith gives us the self-assurance we can come to God and seek His pardon.

Verse 21 is an antecedent, for John next reminds and instructs us on how to properly petition God for answers to prayer. He wants us to acknowledge *why* we received God's grace and love.

Answers - 1st John 3:22-24

And whatever we ask we receive from Him, because we keep His commandments and do those things that are pleasing in His sight.

And this is His commandment: that we should believe on the name of His Son Jesus Christ and love one another, as he gave us commandment.

1ˢᵗ John 3:22–23

We must believe Christ is our savior and that only through Him we have salvation and eternal life. We must have exhibited this faith by loving others as Christ and God have loved us with the granting of the great endowment of deliverance. If these two factors – belief and loving others – are present, then we shall receive, if what we request is of God's will and will bring glory to Him, whatever we ask.

The answering of our prayers is not a reward. It is done because of our faith in Christ for our salvation and our adherence to His commandment to love. Meeting these two conditions puts us in His will. By being in His will our prayers will be correct in nature and intent. Our prayer requests must always be that when answered the glory will be given to God. Not only should we acknowledge whatever favor is granted is done so by God, but we must be certain others see His provision in our lives. We must proclaim to the world that what we receive is from the hand of God. This kind of quiet witness is more powerful, in most cases, than a fiery sermon or arm-twisting witness.

Let's take these two verses apart. The words and phrases in them are powerful and need to be closely examined. In verse 22 we need to correctly define "whatever.'

Depart from evil and do good; Seek peace and pursue it.

The eyes of the Lord are on the righteous, And His ears are open to their cry.

Psalms 34:15

God sees us, if we are righteous, no matter where we are. He knows about our good lives and hears our call. Of course, it helps that He is omniscient and has foreknowledge of what is to befall us, but generally when we cry to Him, it is not a surprise.

> *He does not withdraw His eyes from the righteous; But they are on the throne with kings, For he has seated them forever, And they are exalted.*

Job 36:7

In the Book of Job, historically the oldest portion of scripture in existence, one of Job's "comforters," Elihu, makes this comment. In the irony of the book he is not trying to reassure Job but is trying to shame Job into admitting he has done something terribly wrong to have received the punishment he has from God. Actually Job is not guilty of any transgression, and the lesson taught is that God is all-powerful and we as His creation have no right to question His judgments on us. Yet the statement Elihu makes here is true, only it needs to be expanded. God is observing us all always, no matter what our station in life. The LORD cares for those who worship and honor Him. The catch is that not receiving glory and honor is ***not*** an automatic divine condemnation. Our rewards may not come on this plane of existence. Nevertheless, our daily living should be such that we anticipate the splendor we will receive when we join Christ in the heavens at the time of our death.

> *Behold, the eye of the Lord is on those who fear Him, On those who hope in His mercy,*

Psalms 33:18

David continues this theme in Psalm 33. It should be our comfort as we plow through the burdens of daily life that our God sees how we are living and serving. How heartening to realize the LORD knows when we do those things that please Him. This "fear" is not the dread or terror pagans associated with the presence of their deities. In the Judeo-Christian concept it is an awe, an admiration, a spirit of wonder and amazement. "Hoping in His mercy" is a way of saying by righteous living we trust our faithfulness will be rewarded. Naturally, it is.

> *'And he who sent Me is with Me. The Father has not left Me alone, for I always do those things that please Him.'*

John 8:29

Christ spoke these words, and they need to be a model for our lives. These words were His "human" understanding of His "divine" purpose. As His followers, we share the same objective. An absolute personal commitment that the LORD is present with us – through the indwelling of the Holy Spirit – and that He has not left us, gives us confidence our actions, words, deeds and attitudes are in alignment with God and His purposes.

In verse 22, the verb *"ask"* along with its conjunctive *"whatever"* need to be properly understood to avoid false expectations. The Greek rendering of *"whatever"* would be "if, in case." This limits the results to the specifics of our request, not a blanket response. Sincere prayer requests must be precise. Yes, the LORD's omniscience makes Him aware of our needs, but we carefully analyze our circumstances before we seek divine guidance. This eliminates frivolous petitions born out of misguided thoughts "Ask" is defined as *"to beg, call for, crave, desire, require."* It is a request from one of a lower state of one in higher authority. It is an insistent appeal but without qualms because the questioner knows the granter longs to provide what is sought. Understand this is conditional on the steadfastness of our faith. Since one properly united in Spirit with Christ would only be seeking those things worthy, valuable and significant for the furtherance of His Kingdom, the things we *beg for, call for, crave, desire, or require* would be in alignment with God's will, and not the pointless, useless cravings of our human nature. Look at how Jesus originally taught this concept to John:

> *'Ask, and it will be given to you; seek, and you will find; knock, and it will be opened to you.*

'For everyone who asks receives, and he who seeks finds, and to him who knocks it will be opened.

'Or what man is there among you who, if his son asks for bread, will give him a stone?

'Or if he asks for a fish, will he give him a serpent?

'If you then, being evil, know how to give good gifts to your children, how much more will your Father who is in heaven give good things to those who ask Him!

'Therefore, whatever you want men to do to you, do also to them, for this is the Law and the Prophets.

'Enter by the narrow gate; for wide is the gate and broad is the way that leads to destruction, and there are many who go in by it.

'Because narrow is the gate and difficult is the way which leads to life, and there are few who find it.

Matthew 7:7–14

This is a latter portion of the "Sermon on the Mount." Historically it is not likely that the text in Matthew 5-7 was "preached" all at one time. Rather, it is a compilation by Matthew of teachings and sayings from the three years of Christ's ministry. It encapsulates the essence of what Jesus wanted us to know, and is definitely a magnificent summation of what living a godly life is all about.

When one reads this section, it is clear how John then boiled down the words to his passage in 1ˢᵗ John 3:22-23. The second portion of the passage is a commandment, a familiar commandment, from Jesus – known not only to His followers, but to Jews, and to the readers of this epistle from John:

'And the second is like it: "You shall love your neighbor as yourself.'

Matthew 22:39

119

Jesus is quoting, in response to the question of which is the greatest commandment, Leviticus 19:18:

> *'You shall not take vengeance, nor bear any grudge against the children of your people, but you shall love your neighbor as yourself: I am the Lord.*

> *Leviticus 19:18*

But note there is a second portion of this commandment, presented as an antecedent to this phrase. It was intended for the Hebrews of ancient times, so to the Jews of Christ's days it hardly seemed relevant. Their daily lives were controlled by the hated occupiers, the Romans, and passive resistance, or aggressive like that of the Zealots, was seen as a way of keeping the feeling of ethnic unity alive. Yet Jesus, quoting only the second part of the passage for Leviticus and knowing His listeners knew what came before it, makes a powerful point. *Love means accepting that the ultimate justice will be executed by the LORD,* so our nature must be one of brotherhood and love.

> *Vengeance is Mine, and recompense; Their foot shall slip in due time; For the day of their calamity is at hand, And the things to come hasten upon them.'*

> *Deuteronomy 32:35*

This was God's promise to the Jews of Moses" time; knowing Him to be unchanging, the crowd hearing Jesus' response knew this promise was still in effect. And, with the assurance the matter would be dealt with properly and divinely, they could and should concentrate on righteous living.

To be certain, the Jews, and we, see that peaceful living is possible when we turn the burden of punishment over to God. This concept is reiterated over and over again.

> *Vengeance is Mine, and recompense; Their foot shall slip in due time; For the day of their calamity is at hand, And the things to come hasten upon them.'*

> *Deuteronomy 32:35*

Moses reassures the Jews God *will* execute judgment on those who deserve it; they should focus on loving one another.

> *'Let the Lord judge between you and me, and let the Lord avenge me on you. But my hand shall not be against you.'*

> *1ˢᵗ Samuel 24:12*

David shouts across a valley to his enemy King Saul that, though he (David) had the opportunity to kill Saul, to end his persecution at Saul's hand, and claim the throne of Israel as God had promised. But David chose to allow God to handle the matter.

> *Beloved, do not avenge yourselves, but rather give place to wrath; for it is written, "Vengeance is Mine, I will repay," says the Lord.*

> *Romans 12:19*

Paul, who had many reasons to seek revenge on those who had harmed, betrayed and threatened him, urges the church in Rome not to strike against those who persecute it. Paul knew his Old Testament, and knows his readers do, too, as he quotes the Leviticus passage.

Christ amplifies the Leviticus passage as he presents what should be the proper response to our mistreatment at the hands of others:

> *'You have heard that it was said, "You shall love your neighbor and hate your enemy.'*

> *'But I say to you, love your enemies, bless those who curse you, do good to those who hate you, and pray for those who spitefully use you and persecute you,*

> *'that you may be sons of your Father in heaven; for he makes His sun rise on the evil and on the good, and sends rain on the just and on the unjust.*

> *'For if you love those who love you, what reward have you? Do not even the tax collectors do the same?*

> *'And if you greet your brethren only, what do you do more than others? Do not even the tax collectors do so?*

> *'Therefore you shall be perfect, just as your Father in heaven is perfect.*
>
> **Matthew 5:43–48**

He concludes with the commendation of our behavior we will receive if we respond in this way. To grasp the broader picture, understand that "*perfect*" really means *to be brought to its end, finished; wanting nothing necessary to completeness; consummate human integrity and virtue of men, all grown, adult, of full age, mature.* This is certainly far from our concept of "without blemish or defect." That is an important distinction when looking at biblical standards of perfection. Grasping that biblical "perfection" is a measure of completion and not of performance should ease the stress many feel as they try to "measure up" to godly standards.

All this to point out the elemental center of God's law is love.

> *Owe no one anything except to love one another, for he who loves another has fulfilled the law.*
>
> *For the commandments, "You shall not commit adultery," "You shall not murder," "You shall not steal," "You shall not bear false witness," "You shall not covet," and if there is any other commandment, are all summed up in this saying, namely, "You shall love your neighbor as yourself.'*
>
> *Love does no harm to a neighbor; therefore love is the fulfillment of the law.*
>
> **Romans 13:8–10**
>
> *For as many as are of the works of the law are under the curse; for it is written, "Cursed is everyone who does not continue in all things which are written in the book of the law, to do them.'*
>
> **Galatians 3:10**

For whoever shall keep the whole law, and yet stumble in one point, he is guilty of all.

James 2:10

Put these three passages together and one sees if one wishes to live a life in agreement with God's fundamental laws, there is no alternative to loving others unconditionally. The conclusion James and Paul reach is that failure to get any point of the law is failure to keep any of it. They both admit Christ's sacrifice satisfied that demand, but our commitment should be to live loving others, and that commandment is the most important one.

The charge of Leviticus 19:18 is "the old commandment." But Christ's "New Commandment" is an extension and elaboration of it, moving beyond the literal meaning to include __all__ our relationships, not just the one with the heavenly Father. It is this broadening of the concept of "loving" that is distinctive about Christianity. No other religion or culture of the world has this characteristic. In every other religious system there is provision for willful destruction of those not a part of it.

John closes this chapter with a reassuring summation.

Now he who keeps His commandments abides in Him, and he in him. And by this we know that he abides in us, by the Spirit whom he has given us.

1st John 3:24

One who keeps and practices Jesus' teaching, especially those instructions related to loving others, is in His care. Christ's power and our life-likeness of Him are part of us. We have proof of this by the presence and operation of the Holy Spirit in us. Allowing our lives to led by the Spirit produces the unmistakable fruit of the spirit, loving one another.

Jesus answered and said to him, "If anyone loves Me, he will keep My word; and My Father will love him, and We will come to him and make Our home with him.

John 14:23

Jesus promises anyone who loves Him and follows His commandments ('*keep My word*') will be loved by the Father. That one will also receive the blessing and presence of the Holy Spirit ('*We*')

'By this we know" –

> '*he who has My commandments and keeps them, it is he who loves Me. And he who loves Me will be loved by My Father, and I will love him and manifest Myself to him.*'

> **John 14:21**

Christ will make Himself real in those who persist in adherence to His commandments.

> *And what agreement has the temple of God with idols? For you are the temple of the living God. As God has said: "I will dwell in them And walk among them. I will be their God, And they shall be My people.*'

> **2nd Corinthians 6:16**

We need to define what is meant by "the Spirit." It[11] is that part of a person capable of responding to God's leading and draws us into a stronger communion with Christ. It convicts us of sinful attitudes and acts and convinces us of the acceptability of Christ's sacrifice for our sins. It reassures us of our salvation, counteracting the doubting thoughts placed in our minds by Satan. With all the stress of today's living, it strengthens us as we face daily challenges. The power of scripture is unlocked to our minds by the Holy Spirit. It enables us to pray according to God's will, and gives us the courage to share Christ with others.

God's presence makes that in which He dwells holy and sacred. As He abides in us through the Holy Spirit and the faith in our hearts, then we become "temples" for Him. Paul's quotation expresses the LORD's intent for the ancient Hebrews, but they lacked the permanence of the Holy Spirit, and so relied on the physical Tabernacle to represent God's "home.'

For this reason I bow my knees to the Father of our Lord Jesus Christ,

from whom the whole family in heaven and earth is named,

that he would grant you, according to the riches of His glory, to be strengthened with might through His Spirit in the inner man,

that Christ may dwell in your hearts through faith; that you, being rooted and grounded in love,

may be able to comprehend with all the saints what is the width and length and depth and height

to know the love of Christ which passes knowledge; that you may be filled with all the fullness of God.

Ephesians 3:14–19

In this hymn of praise to God Paul clearly spells out the benefits of having the LORD'S presence in our lives. He has expanded the Old Testament concept of the Almighty to properly include His Son, Christ Jesus our Lord, and the Holy Spirit. Paul states that through faith we are blessed with the presence of the Spirit in our hearts and thereby understand the limitlessness of God's love.

But you are not in the flesh but in the Spirit, if indeed the Spirit of God dwells in you. Now if anyone does not have the Spirit of Christ, he is not His.

Romans 8:9

Paul puts it even plainer and simply in this passage in his Roman epistle. Being a believer and accepting the presence of the Holy Spirit transforms us from ordinary human beings to spiritual representatives of the LORD. We are no longer "fleshly."

For as many as are led by the Spirit of God, these are sons of God.

Romans 8:14

125

This brings us back to the start of this cyclical argument. This loop is a self-fulfilling definition of being filled with the Spirit and it means we exhibit certain characteristics and abilities; having those talents then gives us the privilege of "knowing" Christ. And by "knowing" Christ, we are filled with the Spirit.

But what do we mean by "knowing" Christ? A contemporary sect called the Gnostics, a major challenge to John's teaching, takes its name from the root Greek word *to know*. *Ginosko* means to know through experience, to perceive through "subjective knowledge" from an active relationship between the one who knows and the person or thing known. First hand understanding or unfettered perception is the key. The knowledge gained is the result of observation and participation; in the Gnostic view, one does not accept something as knowable simply because another tells you it is so; it is only legitimate when it is personally verifiable.

So, John ends his third chapter with a circular statement about the presence and the assurance of that presence in believers. He takes a breath and plunges on in Chapter Four.

Further Testing – 1st John 4:1 - 2

J ohn sails right into his next points without so much as a pause. Remember these epistles were read aloud in assemblages of believers, not studied and contemplated by candlelight or while sitting on the shore of some restless sea. Our artificial chapter divisions, while making scripture passages organized, sometimes bear no relevance with the thought train of the writer. John, especially, is not one to whom logical structure held major significance.

Other authors have classified Chapter 4 as having two emphases – life in the family of believers and the certainty of our faith. There are some who place great emphasis on the first six verses as additional criteria for judging the spirits of the world, then assign the remainder of the chapter to refinement of understanding our communion with God. The tempo of the writing seems to have picked up at this point, as though John were realizing he had gone in circles a few times, and now needs to try to wrap everything back together. So, he jumps back to his instruction on how to test the viability of the spirits of those who challenge the core beliefs of Christianity.

> *Beloved, do not believe every spirit, but test the spirits, whether they are of God; because many false prophets have gone out into the world.*
>
> *1ˢᵗ John 4:1*

John uses a Greek verb form that means to commit to a long-term testing of the messages received from other "spirits." The actual word used is "to try," in the sense of proving or to recognize something as genuine after examination, to approve, deem worthy. The second use of the word "spirit" in this verse carries a different connotation; the initial reference is to that of the Spirit of God, the "Holy Spirit." The second use is for any other spirit. The spirits we are to test are the disposition or influence which fills and governs the soul of any one, the efficient source of any power, affection, emotion, or desire.

Let two or three prophets speak, and let the others judge.

But if anything is revealed to another who sits by, let the first keep silent.

For you can all prophesy one by one, that all may learn and all may be encouraged.

And the spirits of the prophets are subject to the prophets.

For God is not the author of confusion but of peace, as in all the churches of the saints.

1ˢᵗ Corinthians 14:29–33

Paul outlines the way a Christian is to manage words spoken as "messages, commands or prophecies" from those claiming anointing of the Holy Spirit. He approves of the concept that there can be multiple voices of spiritual revelations in a worship setting. The directions in verse 30 imply that should another have words that might be contradictory or that challenge the meaning of the first speaker, the initiator should not dispute the new words, but be quiet and allow those in the group to judge by their own spiritual measurement their accuracy or voracity. He explains that the example of the historical prophets is the governance of modern speakers. The key to Paul's direction is that there will be harmony among the words spoken, for "God is not the author of confusion" and the ultimate goal of sharing spiritual revelations is to unite and edify the body of the church. Christ Himself warned in Matthew 24:5, "For many will come in My name, saying, "I am the Christ," and will deceive many."

This is a slight variation of John's earlier warnings about not blindly accepting any and every thing taught by those claiming to represent God. There are many who intentionally wish to spread false teachings; there are many who spread them unintentionally, too. John's cautions are intended to slow down the spread of counterfeit doctrines through patient sifting and evaluation. This is truly a case of knowledge being the weapon to thwart Satan's design.

By this you know the Spirit of God: Every spirit that confesses that Jesus Christ has come in the flesh is of God,

1ˢᵗ John 4:2

John states it plainly: not every one who claims to speak for the Almighty actually does so. A sign or guide of who is a true (and to be believed) teacher is one who confesses that Christ has come to in the flesh. Compare this warning to John's earlier cautions against those who *do not* recognize the human incarnation of Jesus.

that if you confess with your mouth the Lord Jesus and believe in your heart that God has raised Him from the dead, you will be saved.

For with the heart one believes unto righteousness, and with the mouth confession is made unto salvation.

Romans 10:9–10

John stands in agreement with no less an authority the Apostle Paul. Paul, writing to the fellowship in Rome, where false teachers and apostasy flourish, set forth the standard for one to be considered an authentic salvation. The oral confession of Christ's humanity and His bodily resurrection was mandatory.

What were the conditions and benefits of "if we confess?"

'Therefore whoever confesses Me before men, him I will also confess before My Father who is in heaven.

Matthew 10:32

The confession has to be "before men" (*people*). This is frequently emphasized in some congregations as a prerequisite for baptism, a public testimony and admission of Christ as Savior.[12] Why? Because doing so puts the individual in the position of having <u>accountability</u>. They cannot modify or recant their statements at a later time because it has been heard by more than one other set of ears; there cannot be any "he said, she said" with a public confession of faith. But look at the benefit. Christ will "confess" our forgiveness (according one of definitions of "confess" not to deny, declare, to praise, celebrate.)

Jesus is going to come before the Father and tell Him we, personally and individually, have been cleansed of our sins by Christ's atoning death, and we deserve the grace of eternal life in heaven. Isn't that fantastic? Isn't that the most marvelous gift one could ever be given?

> *'Also I say to you, whoever confesses Me before men, him the Son of Man also will confess before the angels of God.*

> *Luke 12:8*

Luke expands that requirement slightly, extending the audience of Christ's confession to the "angels of God." Because the angels seemingly have no concept of sinfulness and the necessity of redemption, the LORD makes human confessions available to them to help educate them as to what His plan of salvation is all about. It is a humbling thought to realize that as you stand before a congregation speaking your testimony of faith to visualize a crowd of heavenly beings floating in the air above you, hanging on every syllable. Again, note though, the emphasis is on a "public" confession, not one done in private that could later have been claimed to be the result of pressure or coercion.

> *So Philip ran to him, and heard him reading the prophet Isaiah, and said, "Do you understand what you are reading?'*

> *And he said, "How can I, unless someone guides me?" And he asked Philip to come up and sit with him.*

> *The place in the Scripture which he read was this: "he was led as a sheep to the slaughter; And as a lamb before its shearer is silent, So he opened not His mouth.*

> *In His humiliation His justice was taken away, And who will declare His generation? For His life is taken from the earth.'*

> *So the eunuch answered Philip and said, "I ask you, of whom does the prophet say this, of himself or of some other man?'*

Then Philip opened his mouth, and beginning at this Scripture, preached Jesus to him.

Now as they went down the road, they came to some water. And the eunuch said, "See, here is water. What hinders me from being baptized?'

Then Philip said, "If you believe with all your heart, you may." And he answered and said, "I believe that Jesus Christ is the Son of God.'

So he commanded the chariot to stand still. And both Philip and the eunuch went down into the water, and he baptized him.

Now when they came up out of the water, the Spirit of the Lord caught Philip away, so that the eunuch saw him no more; and he went on his way rejoicing.

Acts 8:30–38

Luke records in Acts an apparent exception of the "public confession" principle in the story of Philip and the Ethiopian eunuch. Carried by the Spirit to the road where this prince from Africa was traveling, Philip came up into his chariot and helped the man understand what he was reading by explaining the nature of Christ's fulfillment of the prophecies.

The new evangelist immediately realized the sincerity of the Ethiopian, but also recognized the need for enlightenment so he, led by the Spirit, interpreted the Word. As any good preacher would, Philip capitalized on the man's curiosity and acknowledged that, with confession, the Ethiopian could be baptized.

Now, the "before men" stipulation – how was it satisfied in this instance? Remember the Ethiopian was identified as (according to Strong) a prince, a potentate, a courtier, high officer, a royal minister of great authority. He was riding in a chariot and reading aloud. *There had to be a driver.* No doubt there were other attendants accompanying him; he would not have been traveling alone. There were others around while Philip taught. Thus, the "before men" condition was satisfied and the new believer baptized in a convenient pool.

> *For to this end Christ died and rose and lived again,*
> *that he might be Lord of both the dead and the living.*

Romans 14:9

Paul, in his Roman epistle, concisely identifies the content of the confession that is to be made before men. Jesus Christ, the humanly incarnate Son of God, died for our sins on the cross – actually and completely died – but by the power of the Almighty, rose from the dead and again assumes his role as Lord of both those who are living now and to whom He offers the gift of eternal life through faith in Him, and those who have already died. When one compares this claim of divinity against the claims of the other "gods" of the times, Jehovah is the ultimate god. The Greeks, Romans, Egyptians, Babylonians all have gods, but none of them were "ultimate" or all inclusive deities; they were god of the sun or the moon, rivers, mountains, wind, fire. None of the other cultures extant in the first century AD were supreme. There are in Greek mythology many stories of the competition between the different gods. Judaism and Christianity, with their staunch construction of a religion based on a single, all-powerful and compassionate God alone offered hope and redemption to mankind.

Writing to the Corinthians, Paul lays on one more condition of the confession of Christ as Savior:

> *Therefore I make known to you that no one speaking by*
> *the Spirit of God calls Jesus accursed, and no one can*
> *say that Jesus is Lord except by the Holy Spirit.*

1st Corinthians 12:3

And it makes sense. Only one who has received Christ and has been filled with the Spirit (as all are who accept the gift of salvation and believe it) can so proclaim it. It is a circular syllogism: you cannot do "*A*" unless you have "*B*", and if you have "*B*", you can only say "*A*". The circle is locked. And, by God's grace, it cannot be opened.

Is there ever going to be a time when every single individual will acknowledge Christ as Lord? Paul thinks so and speaks of it in his letter to the Philippians.

> *Therefore God also has highly exalted Him and given Him the name which is above every name,*
>
> *that at the name of Jesus every knee should bow, of those in heaven, and of those on earth, and of those under the earth,*
>
> *and that every tongue should confess that Jesus Christ is Lord, to the glory of God the Father.*

> *Philippians 2:9–11*

John's Revelation describes this scene, a time after all the horrendous judgment, trials, and tribulations. When Satan's power is at last destroyed, everyone still living will realize who Jesus was and is. They will drop to their knees, bow their heads and make that public confession that Christ is LORD, as John says must be done in the second verse of the fourth chapter of his first epistle.

Identifying the Antichrist– 1st John 4:3 - 6

I n the next verse John defines, once more, those who cannot make this confession. Until the times he would see later in his Revelation those who do not acknowledge Christ are of the spirit of the Antichrist. John repeats his belief that this Antichrist is an actual physical individual, who will appear. Where there comes challenges to John's thinking is the phrase *"and is now already in the world."* My interpretation is John's concept of *"spirit"* at this point was of the disposition or influence which fills and governs the soul of any one, the efficient source of any power, affection, emotion, desire, etc. I believe the *"is now already"* is referring to the attitude of the Antichrist, and not the individual. Such an interpretation is logical since we do see a spirit of evil all around us, and have seen it since the time of Christ. Certainly such a negative power was not limited to the First Century.

> *and every spirit that does not confess that Jesus Christ has come in the flesh is not of God. And this is the spirit of the Antichrist, which you have heard was coming, and is now already in the world.*

> *1ˢᵗ John 4:3*

American popular writer Joel C. Rosenberg presents an astonishingly simple solution to this confusion. In his novel *The Ezekiel Option* a character points out that even Christ did not know when He was to return; that was knowledge left solely to the Father. If Christ doesn't know the day and hour of His Second Coming, obviously neither does Satan. Since Satan must produce the Antichrist before that glorious event, the Evil One must have available, every minute of every day, a person who could be transformed into the Antichrist. If Christ did not return during their lifetime, they pass on into history as symbols of evil incarnate. Thus, Attila the Hun, Napoleon, Frederick the Great, Hitler, Stalin – all could have been "Antichrist candidates" who were not used.

Taken together, verses 2 and 3 absolutely define what the confession of belief must be. John's reiteration of this point reflects his concern for his "little children." he does not want them to fall prey to evil spirits, to be lead down the wrong path and away from the road of salvation. It is an almost frantic yearning for their faith to be strengthened.

> *You are of God, little children, and have overcome them, because he who is in you is greater than he who is in the world.*

> *They are of the world. Therefore they speak as of the world, and the world hears them.*

> *1ˢᵗ John 4:4–5*

John reassures his readers they are <u>not</u> of this worldly nature. Because they possess the Spirit of Jesus Christ, they are secure.

'*He who is in you is greater than he who is in the world*' has been converted to a popular praise and worship chorus I first heard more than 40 years ago on an Oral Roberts television special. It was my first exposure and my first attraction to the concept of a personal relationship with Jesus Christ. Back then Roberts was working to re-mold his tent evangelistic faith-healing image into a more main stream religious enthusiasm. After founding his university in Tulsa, he began producing highly professional television programs. Excellent singing and dancing troupes were made up of students and popular entertainment figures were guests on his "specials." It was the beginning of the "charismatic movement" but still within the bounds of "safe belief." In fact, Reverend Roberts was granted ordination within the United Methodist Church. It would take several more years, active service in the campus ministry of the United Methodist Church, a patient and prayerful wife, and diligent study in Bible study groups before that relationship fully blossomed in me. But the image of that group of young people, most not much older than I, singing the phrases over and over to the accompaniment of a full orchestra, never left my mind. The seed was definitely planted that night.

The truth of the phrase is not debatable. Acknowledging that the "Ruler of the World" is the Devil, Christ says,

> *'I will no longer talk much with you, for the ruler of this world is coming, and he has nothing in Me.*

> *John 11:30*

He makes it absolutely, positively, crystal-clear that that worldly spirit has nothing in common with God.

> *"he who hears you hears Me, he who rejects you rejects Me, and he who rejects Me rejects Him who sent Me."*

> *Luke 10:16*

Since his readers have no problem acknowledging the world's rejection of them – after all, as John was writing this letter they were suffering unspeakable persecution – they accepted the rejection. It was easy enough to interpolate that denunciation of them individually into denial of Jesus Christ as savior. The comfort was in the recognition of His ultimate power being greater than that of Satan.

There is no difficulty accepting "they" to be those followers of the Antichrist and who have his spirit which, right now, seems to be the whole world. It is a familiar theme for the disciple whom Jesus loved:

> *'he who comes from above is above all; he who is of the earth is earthly and speaks of the earth. he who comes from heaven is above all.*

> *John 3:31*

And the Apostle Paul, too, though he gets a bit long-winded, poetic and complicated is saying the same thing.

> *The first man was of the earth, made of dust; the second Man is the Lord from heaven.*

> *As was the man of dust, so also are those who are made of dust; and as is the heavenly Man, so also are those who are heavenly.*

> *And as we have borne the image of the man of dust, we*
> *shall also bear the image of the heavenly Man.*
>
> *1ˢᵗ Corinthians 15:47-49*

Those who are God's own can and will overcome those belonging (or pledging allegiance) to Satan because Christ's children have the greater power at their disposal. Those refuting His incarnate deity are unsaved and will remain so until they make the confession of Christ as LORD. The world – that population not having Jesus in their hearts – seems to respond to the appeal of the Devil and is drawn to it.

Those who reject Christ as the living Son of God are also rejecting the Lordship of Him in their lives. This invalidates any "prophecy" or "revelation" they might offer. They are false from top to bottom, front to back. But the greater capacity of discernment present in believers girds Christians. Believers have already won the victory and defeated the challenge of false teachings; we just need to be confident in that.

> *We are of God. he who knows God hears us; he who is*
> *not of God does not hear us. By this we know the spirit*
> *of truth and the spirit of error.*
>
> *1ˢᵗ John 4:6*

We Christians acknowledge, believe, obey, hear and accept what the Spirit within us confirms. Those who are not filled cannot and do not understand the message we bring, and we cannot accept what they say. This irrevocable difference separates us. In some cases it is not willful disobedience on the part of the unbeliever, but an inability to comprehend what is being said. Satan will use every means possible to cloud their minds.

> *'he who comes from above is above all; he who is of the*
> *earth is earthly and speaks of the earth. he who comes*
> *from heaven is above all.*
>
> *'And what he has seen and heard, that he testifies; and*
> *no one receives His testimony.*
>
> *'he who has received His testimony has certified that*
> *God is true.*

> *'For he whom God has sent speaks the words of God,*
> *for God does not give the Spirit by measure.*
>
> *John 3:31–34*

This passage from John's gospel not only defines who is a believer, but also one who is not. *"By this"* in 1st John 4:6 is clarified in the letter but also in this passage as one who is from Satan. They speak (or teach) in an earthly manner and of earthly things. One who represents the Spirit speaks (and teaches) of those things associated "above all," both physically and ethically.

> *"You are Israel's teacher,"* said Jesus, *"and do you not understand these things?*
>
> *I tell you the truth, we speak of what we know, and we testify to what we have seen, but still you people do not accept our testimony.*
>
> *I have spoken to you of earthly things and you do not believe; how then will you believe if I speak of heavenly things?*
>
> *No one has ever gone into heaven except the one who came from heaven—the Son of Man.*
>
> *Just as Moses lifted up the snake in the desert, so the Son of Man must be lifted up,*
>
> *that everyone who believes in him may have eternal life.*
>
> *John 3:10-15*

This is a fairly simple explanation from Christ of who He is. He absolutely was the only one to have ever come to Earth from above. Our LORD is in conversation with Nicodemus, the Pharisee who came secretly to Jesus at night so as to better grasp the impact of his teaching. One can imagine the incredulity and the sorrow Nicodemus felt as he heard Christ's words in verse 10. Here was one charged with teaching the nation of Israel of the nature of God and he had no true comprehension of the subject.

It is likely Christ's reference to one who has "gone into heaven" reflects His personal freedom of movement from the heavenly realm throughout history. It also can indicate that until His work of redemption was completed there had been no soul to be granted the eternal life reward He now offered. The identity of that person had been a question for some time. Look at Proverbs 30.

> *Who has gone up to heaven and come down?*
> *Who has gathered up the wind in the hollow of his hands?*
> *Who has wrapped up the waters in his cloak?*
> *Who has established all the ends of the earth?*
> *What is his name, and the name of his son?*
> *Tell me if you know!*

Proverbs 30:4

It reads like a pretty good description of the Almighty and His Son.

> *But the righteousness that is by faith says: "Do not say in your heart, "Who will ascend into heaven?" (that is, to bring Christ down)*
>
> *or "Who will descend into the deep?" (that is, to bring Christ up from the dead).*
>
> *But what does it say? "The word is near you; it is in your mouth and in your heart," that is, the word of faith we are proclaiming:*
>
> *That if you confess with your mouth, "Jesus is Lord," and believe in your heart that God raised him from the dead, you will be saved.*

Romans 10:6–9

Paul asserts there is no need for anyone being taught the Word of God to wonder who has descended from heaven and who will ascend to heaven; that knowledge is already dwelling within them if they have made that confession of faith.

> *We are from God, and whoever knows God listens to us; but whoever is not from God does not listen to us.*

> *This is how we recognize the Spirit of truth and the spirit of falsehood.*
>
> *1ˢᵗ John 4:6*

John sums up once more his criteria for determining the veracity of one claiming to speak the Word of God. It, again, is a self-fulfilling circular argument. Follow it backward: If a listener isn't convinced by the words of a speaker about Christ, then that teacher is not filled with the Spirit of God. If the teachings do bring about conviction in the spirit of a believer, then the teacher is part of the fellowship of believers and represents God and His Holiness.

> *I marvel that you are turning away so soon from Him who called you in the grace of Christ, to a different gospel,*
>
> *which is not another; but there are some who trouble you and want to pervert the gospel of Christ.*
>
> *But even if we, or an angel from heaven, preach any other gospel to you than what we have preached to you, let him be accursed.*
>
> *As we have said before, so now I say again, if anyone preaches any other gospel to you than what you have received, let him be accursed*
>
> *Galatians 1:6–9*

Paul has heard of the seeming abandonment of the true Gospel by the church in Galatia. They seemingly had moved into the camp of the Gnostics. He is shocked and profoundly displeased. This letter was written much earlier than 1ˢᵗ John, so our apostle is no doubt aware of the curse cast down on unbelievers by Paul in this passage. The offense was grievous. It threatened the entire legitimacy of Christianity. It had to be stopped. One of John's purposes in writing his letter was to halt this evil spread of Gnosticism in the congregations. It was a major concern for the early church.

Divinity and humanity could not coexist in the same body, according to the Gnostics. In order to acknowledge Christ's teachings and His miracles, Gnostics had to explain how they could emanate from a human, so this absurd theory was concocted. It was that the Spirit of God descended on Jesus when He was baptized, but departed and ascended back to heaven at the instant of His death on the cross. The outlandish precepts of Gnosticism challenge the essence of Christianity. In today's light we can see the foolishness of Gnosticism, but in the first century, everything was new. The struggle to overcome the Gnostic prevalence occupied the majority of the time of the first evangelists of Christianity.

Loving and Living (Part Two) – 1st John 4:7 - 10

J ohn again shifts his thoughts to what turn out to be the major theme of this first epistle.

> *Beloved, let us love one another, for love is of God; and everyone who loves is born of God and knows God.*

1st John 4:7

We should practice loving one another because such affection is "out of," or emanating from, God. If you love others, you are born "of God." If you are born "of God," you know Him. It's that familiar circular logic of which John is so fond. *If A=B and B=C, then C=A.*

John's explanation of the nature of love is not his originally. It is a cornerstone teaching of First Century Christianity and is a common thread throughout the New Testament. Love is commanded by God (as explained in verse 21). Loving one another was commanded by Christ.

> *"A new commandment I give to you, that you love one another; as I have loved you, that you also love one another.*

John 13:34

> *'This is My commandment, that you love one another as I have loved you.*

John 15:12

It doesn't get any clearer or more essential than that. When the Savior tells you He expects it, there is no alternative. Of course, the challenge to the idea is whether the One making the demand had the authority to do so.

Jesus not only taught us this principle of unconditional love, but He lived it.

> *'A new commandment I give to you, that you love one another; as I have loved you, that you also love one another.*

> **John 13:34**

The disciples, having been with Him for three years, had personally experienced His affection for them. They knew, as He said this to them and they walked from the Upper Room to the Garden, that His love for them was genuine.

Paul reinforced the idea when he wrote to the church in Ephesus years before John wrote his epistle.

> *And walk in love, as Christ also has loved us and given Himself for us, an offering and a sacrifice to God for a sweet-smelling aroma.*

> **Ephesians 5:2**

And Paul carried on the teaching in other letters he wrote to other congregations.

> *But concerning brotherly love you have no need that I should write to you, for you yourselves are taught by God to love one another;*

> **1ˢᵗ Thessalonians 4:9**

But even Paul recognized this was not something he needed to preach sermons or give lessons in; it should be a natural part of our being, since we have been created by God and are made in His image. Paul reminds believers in Galatia of the overriding exhibition of love in their lives.

> *For in Christ Jesus neither circumcision nor uncircumcision avails anything, but faith working through love.*

> **Galatians 5:6**

Paul's powerful explanation of the "fruits of the Spirit" includes love.

> *But the fruit of the Spirit is love, joy, peace, long suffering, kindness, goodness, faithfulness,*
>
> **Galatians 5:22**

> *We give thanks to the God and Father of our Lord Jesus Christ, praying always for you,*
>
> *since we heard of your faith in Christ Jesus and of your love for all the saints;*
>
> *because of the hope which is laid up for you in heaven, of which you heard before in the word of the truth of the gospel,*
>
> *which has come to you, as it has also in all the world, and is bringing forth fruit, as it is also among you since the day you heard and knew the grace of God in truth;*
>
> *as you also learned from Epaphras, our dear fellow servant, who is a faithful minister of Christ on your behalf,*
>
> *who also declared to us your love in the Spirit.*
>
> **Galatians 1:3–8**

The Apostle Peter writes of how purity of heart leads to love.

> *Since you have purified your souls in obeying the truth through the Spirit in sincere love of the brethren, love one another fervently with a pure heart,*
>
> *1ˢᵗ Peter 1:22*

His contention is love is the direct, and almost unconscious, result of our cleansed hearts.

The Old Testament prophet Jeremiah recognized the concept that a restored relationship with the LORD would create a new heart, and a new spirit.

"Behold, the days are coming, says the Lord, when I will make a new covenant with the house of Israel and with the house of Judah

not according to the covenant that I made with their fathers in the day that I took them by the hand to lead them out of the land of Egypt, My covenant which they broke, though I was a husband to them, F23 says the Lord.

"But this is the covenant that I will make with the house of Israel after those days, says the Lord: I will put My law in their minds, and write it on their hearts; and I will be their God, and they shall be My people.

Jeremiah 31:31-33

Upon genuine repentance God will place in believers a new heart ('a pure heart," according to Peter). On that heart will be engraved God's law and principles, meaning our nature will become His nature. Since His nature is unconditional love, our nature will take on that aspect. Admittedly, humans have a difficult time loving unconditionally all the time as he does, but we do have the capacity, according to Jeremiah, to do so.

He who does not love does not know God, for God is love.

1ˢᵗ John 4:8

John states it plainly and simply: God is love. We've talked about how one exhibits love, how one performs love, but is there any concrete definitions of "love?" Modern English dictionaries have a seemingly endless list but scriptures provide a much clearer picture of "love's" true nature, of *agape's* nature.

"Agape" is the Greek word used in the New Testament to describe sacrificial, totally accepting, unconditional affection of one for another. It is the love that enabled the early Christians to sell their personal belonging so they could give the proceeds to those needing money. Or to offer their own lives as a sacrifice that another might live. Such love can only be exhibited by one who realizes rewards are not always earthly. *Agape* is the essence of Matthew 22:39 and, consequently, of Leviticus 19:18 – "loving your neighbor as you love yourself.'

> *In this the love of God was manifested toward us, that God has sent His only begotten Son into the world, that we might live through Him.*
>
> *1ˢᵗ John 4:9*

This is a paraphrase of Jesus' explanation to Nicodemus in John 3:16.

> *"For God so loved the world that he gave His only begotten Son, that whoever believes in Him should not perish but have everlasting life."*
>
> *John 3:16*

The LORD'S plan from the very beginning was to restore us to fellowship with Him by offering His Son as a blood sacrifice for us. Humanly, we cannot fathom the depth of that gift. But God did it solely because He wanted us to be sanctified in order to be drawn to Him and into His presence forever. The staggering nature of the gift is compounded even further when Paul explains,

> *But God demonstrates His own love toward us, in that while we were still sinners, Christ died for us.*
>
> *Romans 5:8*

The sacrifice was made while we were still in an unsaved state! It would have been much more logical for us to have expressed repentance and sought a means of forgiveness and then be given the gift of grace. But God made the ultimate gift of the life of His Son even before that, *while we were still sinners.*

> *For unto us a Child is born, Unto us a Son is given; And the government will be upon His shoulder. And His name will be called Wonderful, Counselor, Mighty God, Everlasting Father, Prince of Peace*
>
> *Isaiah 9:6*

The Old Testament prophet Isaiah defines who the "Son" will be in this familiar passage. It is the Messiah of the Hebrews, the One who will triumph over all and bring the world into a rule of righteousness. Isaiah is also describing a political solution to military dominance.

"The Mighty God" is God incarnate, the Omnipotent One, and the God who ultimately triumphs over Satan. He is the victorious one of John's Revelation.

'The Everlasting Father" is the One of gentle, continuous loving care, compassion, and concern.

'The Prince of Peace" is the One reigning over a world of *shalom* (well-being, prosperity, good health, happiness and a cessation of enmity). This Prince, too, shall triumph over the Devil.

Who is "the Son" of 1ˢᵗ John 4:9? According to Strong's[13] Concordance, the word translated "Son" (#5207) is the Greek word Huios. The word is generally used of the offspring of men and in a restricted sense, the male offspring (one born by a father and of a mother). But in a wider sense, "the Son" means a descendant, one of the posterity of anyone, such as the children of Israel. The phrase "son of man" is used by Christ himself, doubtless in order that He might suggest His Messiah-ship and also that He designate Himself as the head of the human family, the man, the one who both furnished the pattern of the perfect man and acted on behalf of all mankind. Christ seems to have preferred this to the other Messianic titles, because by its lowliness it was least suited to fuel the expectation of an earthly Messiah in royal splendor. The term is used predominantly of Jesus Christ as enjoying the supreme love of God, united to Him in affectionate intimacy, privy to His saving councils, obedient to the Father's will in all his acts.

And what is a sinner?

> *let him know that he who turns a sinner from the error of his way will save a soul from death and cover a multitude of sins.*
>
> **James 5:20**

Briefly James describes a "sinner" as one whose soul faces death. The word used for "sinner" describes one devoted to sin, not free from sin, predisposed to sinful living, wicked. It refers to all iniquitous men, specifically of men stained with certain definite vices, reputation, or crimes, such as tax collectors and the heathen. The Old Testament connotation of "sinning" is derived from athletics, wherein one misses the mark, falls short of the goal or target. James' use implies an intentional, deliberate avoidance of seeking the intended point. Another analogy possible from James is of a traveler who leaves the pathway—one who has made a consistent and intentional re-direction of their life, contrary to Christ's standards.

The word "*sent*" in 1st John 4:9 is significant. The verb carries additional portent. The word *Apostello* (Strong #: 649)[14] means to order (one), to go to a place appointed, and to send away, to perform an appointed task. This act of service would be unique. An *Apostello* (note the root of the word "apostle?") was to fulfill a designated task but doing so fully equipped with blessing, backing and authority of the sender. Christ carried on the thread when he made His Twelve the "fishers of men."

> *In this is love, not that we loved God, but that he loved us and sent His Son to be the propitiation for our sins.*
>
> *1st John 4:10*

The rendering here can be confusing. A basic English translation reads "*And this is love, not that we had love for God, but that he had love for us, and sent his Son to be an offering for our sins.*" My own paraphrase is "Pure love is shown to us by God's loving us even though we didn't love Him, and by His providing a counterbalance to our sins through the sacrifice of His Son." The thought is that what was done for us by the LORD was done *in advance*. The propitiation (a fancy word for an appeasing, the means of providing the compensation) for our sins was Christ. God's system of justice, established in the Old Testament, required blood sacrifice for sinful behavior and acts. God is unchanging so that condition could not be set aside. But through Christ's death, once and for all, the requirement was satisfied; every sin of everyone who believed in Jesus would be covered. But the offering was made ***before*** we'd confessed, before we'd acknowledged it. That's the astonishing point of this verse. The gift was made without our having to do anything beforehand.

This verse is another definition of God's love. The unspeakable gift was made for our sakes; there was no advantage for God. His justifiable and legitimate wrath for our sinful acts was met by Jesus' life and death.

> *But when the kindness and the love of God our Savior toward man appeared,*
>
> *not by works of righteousness which we have done, but according to His mercy he saved us, through the washing of regeneration and renewing of the Holy Spirit,*

> **Titus 3:4–5**

Paul's beautiful "*washing of regeneration*" expresses poetically yet realistically what happened at the Incarnation. That baptism purified us; we have been renewed. This new birth is reinforced by the presence of the Holy Spirit, directing our daily lives. We now are serving God and His kingdom.

By the "*renewing of the Holy Spirit*" Paul means the new birth in us replaces our old sinful, human nature. The intent of our living is now not for ourselves; no longer doing the things of the world. Such an existence no longer matters to us. With this new presence, our goal is the reward of eternal life which we have been promised. This fresh lifestyle may not be physically apparent, but it is manifested in our spiritual consciousness.

Becoming a believer involves two steps – the *washing of* regeneration and *renewing of the Holy* Spirit. Baptism is the outward, physical sign of the washing away and rebirth of us as believers. It signals the arrival of the Holy Spirit in our lives and His presence in our lives. The *renewing of the Holy Spirit* is evidenced in the new life of the faithful; the gift of eternal life is ours when we reach that plateau.

This act of renewal, rebirth, was not accomplished by our words or even our righteous deeds. Nothing on our part was a motivation.

The change in our hearts is achieved by the direction of the Holy Spirit in us.

> *Therefore we conclude that a man is justified by faith apart from the deeds of the law.*
>
> *Or is he the God of the Jews only? Is he not also the God of the Gentiles? Yes, of the Gentiles also,*
>
> *since there is one God who will justify the circumcised by faith and the uncircumcised through faith.*
>
> *Romans 3:28–30*

Paul, writing to the Romans, uses the analogy of the Hebrew custom of *physical* circumcision to describe what has occurred to believers *spiritually*. It is real, it happens; the recipient of the rite knows it and is reminded of it every day. But it will not be obvious to the world around them unless the believer lives a life reflective of the change. Customs and decency require that men do not share on a casual basis the fact whether they are circumcised or not, so actions and attitudes must reflect the significance of the commitment it represents.

Christ Himself established the conditions upon which one could become a part of the heavenly citizenship. He spoke with Nicodemus, one of the Pharisees, in a private conference one night in Jerusalem. The words He uses are simple and yet poetic; for believers they are easy to understand and to grasp. But, as is seen in the passage, for someone like Nicodemus who has not accepted Christ as Savior they are stumbling blocks, undecipherable and confusing.

> *Jesus answered and said to him, "Most assuredly, I say to you, unless one is born again, he cannot see the kingdom of God."*
>
> *"Nicodemus said to Him, "How can a man be born when he is old? Can he enter a second time into his mother's womb and be born?"*

Jesus answered, "Most assuredly, I say to you, unless one is born of water and the Spirit, he cannot enter the kingdom of God.

"That which is born of the flesh is flesh, and that which is born of the Spirit is spirit."

"Do not marvel that I said to you, "You must be born again."

"The wind blows where it wishes, and you hear the sound of it, but cannot tell where it comes from and where it goes. So is everyone who is born of the Spirit."

John 3:3–8

The teaching is for one to be privileged enough to see the face of God, to live forever in heaven with the Father and His Son, one must accept the sacrifice of Christ as payment for sin. In doing so, one is transformed magically and instantaneously, into a new creation, *"born again."* The biblical scholar Scofield identifies it as "regeneration."

The necessity of the new birth grows out of the incapacity of the natural man to "see" or "enter into" the kingdom of God. However gifted, moral, or refined, the natural man is absolutely blind to spiritual truth, and impotent to enter the kingdom; for he can neither obey, understand, nor please God. The new birth is not a reformation of the old nature but a creative act of the Holy Spirit. The condition of the new birth is faith in Christ crucified. Through the new birth the believer becomes a partaker of the divine nature and of the life of Christ Himself.[15]

Thus is explained the complex concept of being "born again," which has taken on such a pop culture definition that anyone suddenly having a personal and dramatic spiritual experience declares themselves to be "born again." For it to be truly valid, it must satisfy the four conditions outlined in Scofield's commentary. Perhaps Jesus and Nicodemus discussed these further; the scriptures do not tell us. But it likely the Jewish religious leader listened with new ears to Christ's messages in the days ahead, having heard for himself the stipulations for believership.

To move beyond verse 4:10, we have to explain the concept identified by the word "*propitiation.*" It is a term normally used in a legal sense – either the actual appeasing or a satisfying of requirements set forth in a contract or judicial decision, or the means by which that is done. John uses it only twice in this letter, in 2:2 and here again in 4:10. In the case of salvation it is the means by which God's wrath for our sinfulness is fulfilled. God's unchanging and unfailing law demanded the shedding of blood as payment for sins. Jesus' death did just that; he was the propitiation. Then, since the terms of the covenant have been met, God can, and does, extend His mercy, grace, and forgiveness to us.

Loving and Living (Part Three)
– 1st John 4:11 - 16

J ohn plunges ahead.

> *Beloved, if God so loved us, we also ought to love one another.*
>
> *1ˢᵗ John 4:11*

Our main purpose in living should be to love each other because of the LORD'S love for us, which He demonstrated clearly and plainly through Christ His Son's life and death. Jesus asks His followers

> *"Should you not also have had compassion on your fellow servant, just as I had pity on you?"*
>
> *Matthew 18:33*

This question comes at the conclusion of the Parable of the Unforgiving Servant. Those hearing it hopefully understood the message that if one is forgiven of something great, then forgiveness of something lesser is absolutely mandatory. The point was so strong that Luke referenced it in his gospel as well.

> *'There was a certain creditor who had two debtors. One owed five hundred denarii, and the other fifty.*
>
> *"And when they had nothing with which to repay, he freely forgave them both. Tell Me, therefore, which of them will love him more?"*
>
> *Simon answered and said, "I suppose the one whom he forgave more." And he said to him, "You have rightly judged."*
>
> *Luke 7:41–43*

It is not the depth of the sin, but the breadth of the forgiveness that should matter in our hearts. If God has shown His love to us so mightily, then we ***must*** extend that identical intensity to our fellow humans.

> *No one has seen God at any time. If we love one another, God abides in us, and His love has been perfected in us.*

> *1st John 4:12*

'To see God" in this passage means to behold, look upon, view attentively, contemplate public performances, of important persons that are looked on with admiration, to view, take a view of, in the sense of visiting, meeting with a person, to learn by looking, to see with the eyes, to perceive. All these definitions imply a close, personal, actual physical relationship. John wants his little children to know that such is possible. This places us on a plane with Moses who only got to behold God's "backside" as he passed by.

> *By faith [Moses] forsook Egypt, not fearing the wrath of the king; for he endured as seeing Him who is invisible.*

> *Hebrews 11:27*

But if we have God remaining, sojourning, tarrying, not departing, continuing to be present, held and kept continually in our lives, so we remain as one, not to become another or different. We are assured we shall have an even greater blessing. We will be able to see Him fully and live eternally with Him and His Son.

In his first letter to young Timothy, Paul sings the praise of such a Divinity.

> *Now to the King eternal, immortal, invisible, to God who alone is wise, be honor and glory forever and ever. Amen.*

> *1st Timothy 1:17*

Paul continued,

> *I urge you in the sight of God who gives life to all things, and before Christ Jesus who witnessed the good confession before Pontius Pilate,*

that you keep this commandment without spot, blameless until our Lord Jesus Christ's appearing,

which he will manifest in His own time, he who is the blessed and only Potentate, the King of kings and Lord of lords,

who alone has immortality, dwelling in unapproachable light, whom no man has seen or can see, to whom be honor and everlasting power. Amen.

1ˢᵗ Timothy 6:13–16

Our God is invisible. He is unchallengeable. He dwells in an existence of unapproachable light

he reveals deep and secret things; he knows what is in the darkness, And light dwells with Him.

Daniel 2:22

But this is a light that cannot be seen by ordinary men; only those who have come to Him through His Son's sacrifice will be granted that favor. This concept of "invisibility" to the unbeliever John strikes again in verse 20.

By this we know that we abide in Him, and he in us, because he has given us of His Spirit.

1ˢᵗ John 4:13

God has given us the Holy Spirit, and because He has, we know we are abiding in Him. We know this is true because His Spirit abides in us. Does that sound familiar?

'At that day you will know that I am in My Father, and you in Me, and I in you.

John 14:20

When we recognize Christ's death, sacrifice and resurrection on our behalf, we realize this unique mutual relationship between Him and us.

*And we have seen and testify that the Father has sent
the Son as Savior of the world.*

1ˢᵗ John 4:14

John was a first-hand witness of this glorious and magnificent
amalgamation. John the Baptist heralded it, Christ proclaimed it, and
John, with the other apostles, promulgated it. The purpose of Jesus being
sent into the world was to save the lost.

*'For God did not send His Son into the world to
condemn the world, but that the world through Him
might be saved.*

John 3:17

In his gospel John records Jesus' words that only through Him would
the world be saved.

*"And she will bring forth a Son, and you shall call His
name Jesus, for he will save His people from their
sins."*

Matthew 1:21

The Gospel of Matthew begins with his recording the prophecies
foretelling of Christ's coming. Matthew wrote with the Jewish
audience in mind, carefully constructing his work to assert the
kingship of Christ and the power of God within Him. His being named
"Jesus" signaled the salvation of His people. The name "Jesus' is a
Greek form of "*Iesous,*" Jesus, "Jehovah is salvation." The Old
Testament reference was one well known to the scribes, Pharisees,
Sadducees, and rabbis,

*Then he cried out against the altar by the word of the
Lord, and said, "O altar, altar! Thus says the Lord:
"Behold, a child, Josiah by name, shall be born to the
house of David; and on you he shall sacrifice the
priests of the high places who burn incense on you, and
men's bones shall be burned on you." "*

1ˢᵗ Kings 13:2

The careful research and analysis of Luke reveals the occasion when Jesus spoke of His purpose. There is an episode after a number of memorable experiences for the disciples. Christ had sent them out on missionary journeys with instructions on how to respond if the message they carried was rejected. He had fed the multitudes. Peter proclaimed Him to be the Messiah. Christ had healed and told parables of the true nature of the Kingdom of God, and welcomed the presence of the innocent little children. Now they came to a settlement that, for whatever reason, chose not to accept His teachings.

> *Now it came to pass, when the time had come for Him to be received up, that he steadfastly set His face to go to Jerusalem,*
>
> *and sent messengers before His face. And as they went, they entered a village of the Samaritans, to prepare for Him.*
>
> *But they did not receive Him, because His face was set for the journey to Jerusalem.*
>
> *And when His disciples James and John saw this, they said, "Lord, do You want us to command fire to come down from heaven and consume them, just as Elijah did?"*
>
> *But he turned and rebuked them, and said, "You do not know what manner of spirit you are of.*
>
> *"For the Son of Man did not come to destroy men's lives but to save them." And they went to another village.*
>
> **Luke 9:51–56**

Luke's words for "saved" in verse 50 means to heal, cure, preserve, keep safe and sound, to rescue one from danger or destruction. There is also the connotation of delivering to one a "new life," to have a "new heart."

The LORD sent His Son initially as salvation for the People of His Covenant, the Hebrews, the Chosen Ones. Ironically, they rejected

Him. But the people of Samaria, the place where Jesus met the woman at the well, did receive him. They gradually abandoned their old idolatry and adopted portions of the Jewish religion.

After the return from the Captivity, the Jews in Jerusalem refused to allow the Samaritans to take part with them in rebuilding the temple, and hence sprang up an open enmity between them. They erected a rival temple on Mount Gerizim, which was destroyed by a Jewish king (B.C. 130). They then built another at Shechem. The bitter hostility between the Jews and Samaritans continued in the time of our Lord: the Jews had "no dealings with the Samaritans."

> *[...]they said to the woman, "Now we believe, not because of what you said, for we ourselves have heard Him and we know that this is indeed the Christ, the Savior of the world."*
>
> ### John 4:42

Their word "savior" meant a deliverer, a preserver, benefactor, a rescuer. One must also understand that the "Savior" is the combination of God the Father and Jesus the Son.

> *'For I have given to them the words which You have given Me; and they have received them, and have known surely that I came forth from You; and they have believed that You sent Me.*
>
> ### John 17:8

In His "High Priestly Prayer"[16] for the disciples following the Last Supper, Christ lets them hear Him tell God of the acknowledgment of His authority by His having taught them "the words" God directed. He had no doubt of their faith in Him at this instant. Remember, at the time of the prayer, Judas had left the group. And though Peter was to later deny Him, the big fisherman had previously declared publicly who Jesus was.

> *Whoever confesses that Jesus is the Son of God, God abides in him, and he in God.*
>
> ### 1st John 4:15

The apostle repeats once more the simple requirements for faith and acceptance of the indwelling of the Spirit and the promise of the accompaniment of the Spirit in our lives. The confession of Christ as LORD is the essential obligation.

> *[...] If you confess with your mouth the Lord Jesus and believe in your heart that God has raised Him from the dead, you will be saved.*
>
> **Romans 10:9**

Paul's instruction to the Roman Christians repeats the further details of confession. It must be <u>public</u>. In that way no one may reverse themselves or claim coercion; the decision was on of free-will. It also serves as an example to others, a suggestion to those still not part of the fellowship.

Perhaps it is also time to clearly define *"believe"* in Paul's writing. "To believe" is to have trust in, faith in, to be <u>fully</u> convinced, to acknowledge and rely on those things in your heart. It is a personal reliance upon and trust that produces obedience and submission

Paul and John are only echoing Christ's conditions for faithfulness.

> *'Therefore whoever confesses Me before men, him I will also confess before My Father who is in heaven.*
>
> **Matthew 10:32**

Again, the emphasis is confession *before men* meaning that one cannot be an "authentic Christian" if one is a "closet Christian." The public adherence is mandatory. This is one reason why in many congregations a public profession is expected. Billy Graham has always required those who accepting Christ at his crusades to come forward. Not only does that make it easier for his team to manage follow-up, but it implements Jesus' own expectations of new believers.

> *I will speak of Your testimonies also before kings, And will not be ashamed.*
>
> **Psalm 119:46**

This elaborate and complex Old Testament Psalm includes in it this proud proclamation of testimony. Authentic faith in God (and, from the New Testament perspective, in Jesus) is to be shared proudly to any and every one with whom we come in contact, whether by deed or by word.

> *And we have known and believed the love that God has for us. God is love, and he who abides in love abides in God, and God in him.*
>
> *1ˢᵗ John 4:16*

John again insists he has personally known and seen Christ's love, and he practices it. His faith in its power is not something John was taught by someone else; it is the direct result of exposure to the *agape* of our LORD. One can feel his emotional emphasis that this love is vital, alive, and real.

John states "God is love" and repeats once more the cyclical nature of abiding. This inner reassurance produces the maturity of spirit in believers.

> *Jesus answered and said to* [Judas, not Iscariot], *"If anyone loves Me, he will keep My word; and My Father will love him, and We will come to him and make Our home with him.*
>
> *John 14:23*

Showing Love in the World – 1st John 4:17 - 21

I n their walking journey from the Upper Room to the Garden on the night of His betrayal, Jesus responded to the question from the other Judas, "How are you going to show yourself to us, but not to the world?" Jesus replies that one must first be willing to accept the gift of God's love signified by the keeping of His commandments (which we know now includes the new commandment to love one another). When that happens the Spirit indwells in the believer. That presence will be felt. It will not necessarily be a visible manifestation, not something like a physical mark or "brand" such as the pierced ear of a bond slave. Those expecting something physical could be confused or disappointed.

> *Love has been perfected among us in this: that we may have boldness in the day of judgment; because as he is, so are we in this world.*
>
> *1ˢᵗ John 4:17*

Knowing that *agape*, the unconditional love Christ has taught is part of our makeup, we don't have to be (or should not be) afraid or have any fear of the judgment by the LORD. Positionally, we are the same as Christ. His nature is our nature. We appear to God as He appears to God. He is acceptable, we are acceptable.

And earlier John had written

> *But whoever keeps His word, truly the love of God is perfected in him. By this we know that we are in Him.*
>
> *1ˢᵗ John 2:5*

By "perfected" John means complete, able to carry through completely, to accomplish, finish, bring to an end. Our consecrated lives can bring to a close or fulfillment the events and the prophecies of the scriptures

Remember

> *And now, little children, abide in Him, that when he appears, we may have confidence and not be ashamed before Him at His coming.*
>
> *1ˢᵗ John 2:28*

We have freedom in speaking, unreservedness in speech. Filled with the Holy Spirit, we can speak and behave openly, frankly, without concealment, without ambiguity or circumlocution, without the use of figures and comparisons. We are filled with freedom and fearless confidence, cheerful courage, boldness, assurance. We exhibit the deportment by which one becomes conspicuous. This draws attention to us and the truth of faith in God and Christ secures publicity. All of this is a result of our faith and acceptance in Christ's forgiveness and grace.

> *There is no fear in love; but perfect love casts out fear, because fear involves torment. But he who fears has not been made perfect in love.*
>
> *1ˢᵗ John 4:18*

How does "having love" produce in us a boldness that defeats fear? It does because we are not afraid of the outcome of our actions. We show affection and care for others without hesitation because we want to, not because we have to. We don't worry about what will happen to us when we practice loving actions. There is not anxiety about judgment of us.

Fear is normally associated with punishment. We know we shall not be punished by God, the ultimate Judge, because we have been granted salvation and grace through faith in His Son, our Savior, Jesus Christ. Not facing any negative verdict we behave with only the unselfish motivation of doing for others what we would like to have done for us.

Fear is a symptom of "not trusting." Our trust in Christ is total. Because we have accepted what He has done for us, we know He will do for us only the best. Following the leadership of the Holy Spirit means our lives will be guided by His will and we will experience His mercy in everything we do for His purposes.

Fear of our status on the Day of Judgment is replaced by our love, our concern, our dedication to the well-being and salvation of others.

We want them to have what we have. We truly take into our hearts the concern that "none shall perish" and that all shall be saved.

The sense of this verse is if we feel so self-assured and confident of our salvation then all our actions will be directed at serving and caring for others, not ourselves. We don't have a need to care for ourselves; the LORD has promised to do that. That is "serving in love."

> *We love Him because he first loved us.*
>
> 1st ***John 4:19***

John simply states the reason for our fidelity, His devotion. Our natural response to his unnatural act of sacrifice is the only possible reaction. Remembering from verse 10 that Jesus was our *propitiation*, we understand His offering of Himself satisfied all the requirements of blood sacrifice and sin forgiveness. His act released us from our bondage and set us free.

> *If someone says, "I love God," and hates his brother, he is a liar; for he who does not love his brother whom he has seen, how can he love God whom he has not seen?*
>
> 1st ***John 4:20***

Our love for God manifests itself in our love for others. The perfection of love allows us to replace any feelings of dislike with feelings of affection and devotion. We also desire to serve others. The surest testimony we can give of our genuine love of God is our genuine love for others.

Look back at 1ˢᵗ John 2:4. Now the concept of the authenticity of our relationship with Christ moves from keeping the commandments to pro-action. It now takes the form of sacrificial service, a pale imitation of His sacrificial death. Now the visible lack of love for others in one's life is the signal the testimony of *"I love God"* is false.

This parallels the Old Testament teaching if one desires to know God, one must keep His commandments. Proclaiming that desire without the effort marks one as a liar. How many times have we cited Leviticus 19:18? From the Old Testament all the way through to John's final epistles the message is clear – failure to love our neighbors as we love ourselves is the clear sign we make a mockery of God's law and cannot claim membership in His kingdom. What credibility does one have if they claim to love God (whom they cannot see) but not show love for fellow brothers and sisters whom they can see?

> *And this commandment we have from Him: that he who loves God must love his brother also.*

> *1ˢᵗ John 4:21*

Now the expression of love for others is not merely to be a material manifestation of our affection and devotion to God, but is a commandment. It should be the purpose for which we live. Believers are given the ability to express this superhuman behavior as a natural extension of their transformed lives. It is the total extension of our faith.

Victory Begins – 1st John 5:1–7

John has led us through an amazing string of essential Christian concepts. That's why I consider the First Epistle of John to be an elementary Christian handbook. It touches on and presents the essence of concepts every believer needs to grasp. Combining a reading of the Gospel of John with 1st John will ground any new believer in the faith.

We have studied the necessity for the acceptance of the Incarnation of Christ, God becoming human flesh in order to complete the plan of salvation and grace. We discovered the nature of living a righteous life, and the pattern of the life of the children of God. Finally, we've grasped the nature, the basic of *agape*, the love believers experience and share.

Now, in his final 21 verses, with his rapid-fire and reiterating style, John will tell us of the triumph of righteousness in the world. He will show us the reassurance we have of eternal life. John will conclude his First Epistle with certainties of Christianity. It is an exciting and comforting conclusion to a letter written to offer new and veteran believers knowledge necessary to survive in a morally rapidly declining world. The pace picks up, almost as if John senses time is fleeting as he swiftly reviews his major points.

> *Whoever believes that Jesus is the Christ is born of God, and everyone who loves Him who begot also loves him who is begotten of Him.*

1st John 5:1

Many evangelists toss the phrase "being born again" around incessantly. Its exact definition is often lost in a haze of the conditions a new believer must meet, confusing the issue of the acceptance of Christ's sacrificial death to cover our sins. But John states plainly and simply what believing in Christ actually involves. A believer accepts Christ as lord of his life. Believers love God. They love Christ. And, they love everyone, their neighbors and their enemies. It's that simple.

Christianity means a complete acceptance of others and an exhibition of that *agape* spirit in relationships with them.

Again, one of John's characteristic writing elements, a repetition of previously stated points, is evident. The statement *"Jesus is the Christ"* refers back to 1st John 2:22. Here, though, the emphasis is not on the nature of who He is, but the acceptance of it. If you don't acknowledge it, then you are susceptible to the power of the Antichrist. Being of that negative nature, you cannot love God, Christ or others.

If that's not enough, look back to 4:2. The Spirit of God, which should dwell within believers, confesses to us that the Christ who came in the flesh as God is indeed the Son of God. In 4:15 John asserts anyone who confesses Christ as LORD also abides in and with God, and the LORD dwells within them.

The other key phrase in this verse is *"born of God."* Again, refer back to John 1:13 to see that believers are those <u>not</u> born by blood and by the will of the flesh, but born by the Will of God.

> *having been born again, not of corruptible seed but incorruptible, through the word of God which lives and abides forever,*
>
> *1st Peter 1:23*

Peter affirms the Gospel's point. Those "born again" are done so not through the natural, but the super-naturalism of Christ's redeeming grace. Because of that genesis, a believer's existence will be forever, not subject to the natural laws of decay. We shall live eternally.

> *By this we know that we love the children of God, when we love God and keep His commandments.*
>
> *1st John 5:2*

Loving and obeying God means loving His children. That love of fellow believers is a "reality check" of our love for others; human nature is such there will be some persons easier to accept than others. But to love Him means to love everyone with some level of sincerity.

> *'If you keep My commandments, you will abide in My love, just as I have kept My Father's commandments and abide in His love.*

John 15:10

Jesus tells his disciples in their final walk together that keeping His commandments is a sign and reassurance of their abiding in Him. If we abide in Him, he abides in us.

> *'If you love Me, keep My commandments.*

John 14:15

Jesus says it simply. Now we know that it reads not only as a command but as a description of a Christian.

> *For this is the love of God, that we keep His commandments. And His commandments are not burdensome.*

1ˢᵗ John 5:3

Faith, love and obedience are all interconnected. Loving God means keeping his commandments. The commandments (an order, command, charge, precept, injunction, that which is prescribed to one by reason of his position, a prescribed rule in accordance with which a thing is done, a precept relating to lineage, of the Mosaic precept concerning the priesthood) are difficult to follow. The Greek word used here for "burdensome" is actually "grievous," meaning heavy in weight, or speaking metaphorically, severe, stern, weighty, violent, cruel, unsparing. John says the directions given us by Christ are not hard to follow. Jesus said it first:

> *"For My yoke is easy and My burden is light."*

Matthew 11:30

A "yoke" is the device placed over animals used in farming and hauling. A "light yoke" would be one not involving a great deal of exertion, one easy to manage and not one which is a problem. Jesus says of the artificial rules and regulations created over the centuries by the Pharisees and Sadducees for the people to adhere to,

> *'For they bind heavy burdens, hard to bear, and lay*
> *them on men's shoulders; but they themselves will not*
> *move them with one of their fingers.*

Matthew 23:4

The irony, not missed by Christ, was these requirements were not satisfied by the priests themselves but were imposed upon the common believers. This is a corruption of the nature of The Law. It mocked the nature of God's system. It set up an artificial hierarchy that gave artificial exemption to certain classes. In the LORD'S eyes, <u>everyone</u> is equal, *"all have sinned."*

> *For whatever is born of God overcomes the world. And*
> *this is the victory that has overcome the world-our faith.*

1ˢᵗ John 5:4

The ways of the world will be vanquished by God's faithful. Those faithful are the one who fear Him, obey Him. The most powerful weapon believers have is their faith. Our devotion will ultimately overpower the evil spirits in the world. Though the battle may take ages and at times seem hopeless, we will never be conclusively defeated.

We Christians are the *"whatever is born of God"* and Jesus gave us earlier assurance of our victory.

> *"These things I have spoken to you, that in Me you may*
> *have peace. In the world you will have tribulation; but*
> *be of good cheer, I have overcome the world."*

John 16:33

He did (and has) overcome the world and anything in it.

> *For he Himself is our peace, who has made both one,*
> *and has broken down the middle wall of separation,*

Ephesians 2:14

Paul refers to the walls of the tabernacle which kept the ordinary people away from the place of God. It is possible he also was thinking of the traditional physical separation of males and females during worship services. Whatever he had in mind, the result is the power of Jesus will wipe out these barriers and bring all into one congregation. Paul also says,

> *Yes, and all who desire to live godly in Christ Jesus will suffer persecution.*
>
> *2ⁿᵈ Timothy 3:12*

We believers are victorious over the evil of the world. We face the challenges and tribulations around us every day, but through the power given us by God we prevail. It is not easy but our faith will see us through. Does this mean we will overcome *everything*?

> *Many are the afflictions of the righteous, But the Lord delivers him out of them **all***
>
> *Psalms 34:19* [**Emphasis added**].

Yes, it does. And Paul reassures us, also.

> *Yet in all these things we are more than conquerors through Him who loved us.*
>
> *Romans 8:37*

The road to triumph is not easy, but Jesus is at our side and will walk through it with us. We will walk through the Valley of the Shadow. Together we will reach the end of the trial and the trail.

> *Who is he who overcomes the world, but he who believes that Jesus is the Son of God?*
>
> *1ˢᵗ John 5:5*

Every good teacher asks rhetorical questions. Here is John's in this letter. He's been hammering away the answer off and on for four previous chapters, and through an entire Gospel as well. John answers it himself, but so does Paul.

> *But thanks be to God, who gives **us** the victory through **our** Lord Jesus Christ.*
>
> *1ˢᵗ Corinthians 15:57 [Emphasis added]*

The overcomers of the world are those who believe in Jesus and who have claimed the victory through Christ. These are the steadfast, beloved brethren abounding always with the work of the LORD. Our labor, our struggles, are not in vain. We will win the triumph.

> *This is he who came by water and blood-Jesus Christ; not only by water, but by water and blood. And it is the Spirit who bears witness, because the Spirit is truth.*

> *1ˢᵗ John 5:6*

Jesus, being fully divine as well as fully human, enjoyed the presence of the Holy Spirit all his life. He was not just anointed with Him at his baptism. It did not depart from Him at His Crucifixion.[17] It may seem to be a circular argument, but accept this: We have the same presence of the Holy Spirit. We know it is valid because the Spirit tells us it is so. It is part of our faith to accept this and live with it.

In his gospel, John records,

> *The next day John saw Jesus coming toward him, and said, "Behold! The Lamb of God who takes away the sin of the world!*

> *"This is he of whom I said, "After me comes a Man who is preferred before me, for he was before me."*

> *"I did not know Him; but that he should be revealed to Israel, therefore I came baptizing with water."*

> *And John bore witness, saying, "I saw the Spirit descending from heaven like a dove, and he remained upon Him.*

> *'I did not know Him, but he who sent me to baptize with water said to me, "Upon whom you see the Spirit descending, and remaining on Him, this is he who baptizes with the Holy Spirit.'*

> *"And I have seen and testified that this is the Son of God."*

> *John 1:29–34*

The Baptist's anointing by God was accepted and acknowledged by the people of Israel.

> *Then Jerusalem, all Judea, and all the region around the Jordan went out to him*
>
> *and were baptized by him in the Jordan, confessing their sins.*
>
> *Matthew 3:6*

When Jesus approached him, John the Baptist's announcing His nature was something only that could be revealed to him by the Spirit. If the Spirit did that for John the Baptist, he surely can do the same for us. John the Baptist's witness to those around him that day was *confirmation*, not proclamation. John's declaration was confirmed.

> *And immediately, coming up from the water, he saw the heavens parting and the Spirit descending upon Him like a dove.*
>
> *Then a voice came from heaven, "You are My beloved Son, in whom I am well pleased."*
>
> *Mark 1:10*

Spiritual discernment from the Holy Spirit apart from any human information is a hard concept to grasp. John's recognition of the Christ before his baptism means John the Baptist knew already who the Messiah was.[18] Because the natural (or human) world would acknowledge Him after he was anointed, the Baptist knew the ceremony had to take place, even though he felt unworthy to perform it. It wasn't required for Jesus to be baptized for Him to accomplish His work, but it was needed to convince the people. Today immersion is *not a prerequisite* for salvation, but its performance speaks to unbelievers of one's commitment and acceptance of Jesus as Lord.

The Holy Spirit's presence is central to our faith life. It signals the validity of our belief but it does more than that. Paul, in his letter to the Romans, describes our old situation before the gift of the Spirit.

> *For when we were in the flesh, the sinful passions which*
> *were aroused by the law were at work in our members to*
> *bear fruit to death.*

Romans 7:5

But now with Him having taken residence in us on our profession of faith in Jesus Christ, the Spirit draws us to Christ. We are convicted of sinfulness in our lives by Him (some say this is our conscience). Through the Spirit's power we are able to accept fully Jesus as our personal Lord and Savior and this gives us reassurance of our eternal salvation. With spiritual strength we are able to live a virtuous life. The mental power the Holy Spirit imparts to us enables us to understand scripture and see its true meanings; we are able to pray and discern God's will for ourselves. He enables us to share Christ with others.

John the Baptist told his followers in advance about Jesus.

> *"I indeed baptize you with water unto repentance, but he*
> *who is coming after me is mightier than I, whose sandals I*
> *am not worthy to carry. He will baptize you with the Holy*
> *Spirit and fire."*

> *"His winnowing fan is in His hand, and he will*
> *thoroughly clean out His threshing floor, and gather His*
> *wheat into the barn; but he will burn up the chaff with*
> *unquenchable fire."*

Matthew 3:11–12

Without hesitation John the Baptist testified that "he who came after" would be mightier than himself. And the Baptist felt totally inadequate to serve the Messiah, not even worthy enough to carry His sandals. John's baptisms would be replaced by a baptism by fire *and* water.

Jesus Himself defined who the "son of God" was in a very familiar passage recorded in John.

> *Jesus said to her, "I am the resurrection and the life. he*
> *who believes in Me, though he may die, he shall live.*

'And whoever lives and believes in Me shall never die. ...?'

John 11:25–26

Martha responded that she knew He was the Christ and that He had come to this world to accomplish that of which He spoke.

Before He prayed His Highly Priestly Prayer on the final night with the disciples, Jesus defined for them the Holy Spirit.

'And I will pray the Father, and he will give you another helper, that he may abide with you forever

the Spirit of truth, whom the world cannot receive, because it neither sees Him nor knows Him; but you know Him, for he dwells with you and will be in you.

John 14:16–17

The Holy Spirit is truth, totally truth. It is nothing else. Because of it being such an essence, the world cannot accept the Holy Spirit. Humanity's natural aversion to honesty and integrity makes it absolutely impossible for one so rooted in carnality to recognize and receive the Holy Spirit.

For there are three that bear witness in heaven: the Father, the Word, and the Holy Spirit; and these three are one.

1ˢᵗ John 5:7

If one has doubts about the validity of Christ's purpose, origin, claims, and the legitimacy of the faith, one only has to look to some higher sources for verification. In heaven, the Father, the LORD God Jehovah said it was all true. And Jesus had told His followers, there was no difference between Him and God.

"I and My Father are one."

John 10:30

The Power Within – 1st John 5:8 – 12

The word, the *logos* as John wrote in John 1:1, said it was true. Finally the Holy Spirit, which descended on the disciples at Pentecost and comes into each believer at conversion, says it is true. All these sources corroborate the teachings and the Teacher.

> *And there are three that bear witness on earth: the Spirit, the water, and the blood; and these three agree as one.*
>
> *1ˢᵗ John 5:8*

Here John cites as supporters the like-minded testimony of three disparate sources – the Holy Spirit (existing in each of us), the water (the physical baptism of every believer), and the blood (the sacrificial death of Jesus Christ for our sins.) Together they all point to the same thing: Jesus Christ is LORD and savior. John's gospel explains a bit more of the nature of the Spirit:

> *'But when the helper comes, whom I shall send to you from the Father, the Spirit of truth who proceeds from the Father, he will testify of Me.*
>
> *John 15:26*

Even though some may declare this to be "self-fulfilling prophecy," knowing that the Word of God is truth, these reaffirmations only serve to more fully and firmly establish the nature of Christ. For Jewish purists who demanded the Old Testament standard of two or three witnesses to support a claim

> *'It is also written in your law that the testimony of two men is true.*
>
> *"I am One who bears witness of Myself, and the Father who sent Me bears witness of Me."*
>
> *John 8:17–18*

John trumps this standard by presenting a total of *four* witnesses all agreeing that Jesus Christ is LORD.

> *If we receive the witness of men, the witness of God is greater; for this is the witness of God which he has testified of His Son.*
>
> *1ˢᵗ **John 5:9***

John emphasizes the validity of his message. He's already established that he surpasses the credibility standards acceptable to Mosaic Law. John asserts in addition to that he has the testimony of the Divine.

> *'Yet I do not receive testimony from man, but I say these things that you may be saved.*
>
> *...*
>
> *'And the Father Himself, who sent Me, has testified of Me. You have neither heard His voice at any time, nor seen His form.*
>
> ***John 5:34, 37***

The source of the claims and revelations Jesus made was not from the world, from the carnality of mankind; they were directly from the Almighty. In verse 37 Jesus seemingly challenges those around Him to doubt His claims since they had never, in any way, shape, or form ever had as close communication with Jehovah as He had.

> *'It is also written in your law that the testimony of two men is true.*
>
> *"I am One who bears witness of Myself, and the Father who sent Me bears witness of Me."*
>
> ***John 8:17-18***

Jesus directly states he has satisfied the Old Testament requirement of verification by pointing out that He is one witness, and God is the other. John likely was recalling this quotation as he penned verses 7–9 in his first epistle.

But he was also remembering

And he who has seen has testified, and his testimony is true; and he knows that he is telling the truth, so that you may believe.

John 19:35

Jesus spoke these words to His disciples on that last night together. The word translated into English for *testified* is actually the Greek word for "record." Its meaning was for one a witness, to bear witness, i.e. to affirm that one has seen or heard or experienced something, or that he knows it because taught by divine revelation or inspiration; to give (not to keep back) testimony; to utter honorable testimony, give a good report, conjure, implore The root Greek word is the one from which we derive the English word "martyr." A singular characteristic of a martyr is one who is willing to die for their beliefs. For the disciples and the earlier followers to be willing to suffer death, cruel and uncompromising death, at the hands of the Romans and the Jewish leaders, means there had to be something so compelling to them they were ready to die for its truth rather than compromise and change their stories.

To even further solidify the authenticity of the Christ, recall that God Himself spoke His approval of Jesus at His Baptism. The heavens opened and His voice proclaimed His pleasure, and the dove (representing the anointing of the Holy Spirit) descended to Him.

So, if we do not accept the witness and the testimony of men about Christ, His Kingdom, and the rewarding gift of faith in Him and His sacrifice, we must accept that of God. But God is ultimately behind the witnesses cited in verses 7 and 8 of 1st John Chapter 5.

If we receive the witness of men, the witness of God is greater; for this is the witness of God which he has testified of His Son.

1st John 5:9

Having settled the question of the veracity of the testimony of God and those He has selected to be His witnesses, the question arises: What is it, specifically, that is being testified?

John knows this question would arise, so he introduces his next section by reminding his readers that which is of God is stronger than that which is of man (a concept we'll hit on again shortly).

So, he launches out. First he must reiterate the incongruity of claiming to be a believer when actually not behaving as a believer. "Behavior" applies not only to visible, physical manifestations, but to intellectual and emotional responses.

> *he who believes in the Son of God has the witness in himself; he who does not believe God has made Him a liar, because he has not believed the testimony that God has given of His Son.*

> *1ˢᵗ John 5:10*

John bluntly tells his readers of the very dangerous position someone puts themselves in should they decline to believe in the nature of Jesus. God has said it; God is truth; it must be true. To say it is not true means one is calling God a liar, and that is *definitely* not something one would want to do. Because we have been created in God's image, there is within us a spark of His witness within us.

> *'he who believes in Him is not condemned; but he who does not believe is condemned already, because he has not believed in the name of the only begotten Son of God.*

> *John 3:18*

In His clandestine discourse with Nicodemus, Jesus explains that when our inner witness acknowledges Him, condemnation is passed over us. The implication of *"already"* is now, at this time, presently. This means, because of the curse of Adam, from the moment of our birth we are destined for eternal damnation. Salvation is only available through faith. We have no other choice, we have no other alternative. Our salvation depends on ourselves, on our recognizing Christ as that only sacrifice to justify our transgressions and make us in right standing before God.

> *'he who has received His testimony has certified that God is true.*

> *John 3:33*

Here Jesus says our acceptance of Christ as our savior means we accept God's testimony whether it is through preaching by others, through the pricking of our hearts with our own spirit. This means we declare inwardly, if not to others, as we witness or evangelize, that God is true and what He says is true. By John writing this he is certifying to the world that he, John, is one of those who accepts this. John's witness is verified.

> *And this is the testimony: that God has given us eternal life, and this life is in His Son.*
>
> *1ˢᵗ John 5:11*

We've been laying the groundwork for the validity of the testimony, now what *is* the testimony? It is very simple: God has given us the promise through Jesus of life everlasting in His presence, that death and the grave no longer are our final destination. The testimony is that if we exhibit our faith in the forgiveness of our sins offered by Jesus then we will be spared the pain of being separated from God; instead we will be *with* Him forever.

We need to comprehend what John means by "life." We've all heard the rhetorical question, "What is the meaning of life?" but in this context it is essential to grasp the enormity of the gift being granted. The Greek is *"Zoe."* It means life, the state of one who is possessed of vitality or is animate. This is critical because it means we will be active and functioning; our existence will not be a mental state but an actual physical one. The essence of life is in every living soul.

The life instilled in us by our Creator is one of absolute fullness, both essential and ethical, which belongs to God, and through Him both to the hypostatic "logos" and to Christ in whom the "logos" put on human nature. This eternal life will be real and genuine, a life active and vigorous, totally devoted to God. After our resurrection our "living" will be consummated by new accessions (among them a more perfect body), and it will last forever.

> *he who has the Son has life; he who does not have the Son of God does not have life.*
>
> *1ˢᵗ John 5:12*

What is *"the life"* our friend John speaks of?

'that whoever believes in Him should not perish but have eternal life.

John 3:15

The life is eternal and is granted to those who believe in Christ.

'Most assuredly, I say to you, he who believes in Me has everlasting life.

John 6:47

If "eternal" isn't long enough for you, John quotes Jesus later as saying the life is "everlasting." The Greek word is Aionios, meaning without beginning and end, that which always has been and always will be.

'as You have given Him authority over all flesh, that he should give eternal life to as many as You have given Him.

'And this is eternal life, that they may know You, the only true God, and Jesus Christ whom You have sent.

John 17:2–3

And here is the great reward of that life: the opportunity and ability to "know" God (come to know, get a knowledge of perceive, feel; to become known, to know, understand, perceive, have knowledge of; to understand, to become acquainted with.) That's some relationship.

Let's go back one step and define "believe." It means to be persuaded of, to place confidence in, to trust. It means to have reliance upon, not mere confidence in. *Reliance* implies total dependence on; *confidence* signifies that you could trust in the information but may not count on it to be your total protection and defense.

Returning to the Purpose – 1st John 5:13 – 21

> *These things I have written to you who believe in the name of the Son of God, that you may know that you have eternal life, and that you may continue to believe in the name of the Son of God.*

1ˢᵗ John 5:13

John repeats, for the last time in this letter, his stated purpose in writing. He wants his readers, his little children, his fellow believers, to be reassured of their promised eternal life. That, more than his overcoming the false teachings, rooting out the evil of living a double life, more than challenging the misconceptions of Christ's dual humanity and divinity, John wants believers to rest in the comfort of their future with Jesus and the LORD together in heaven at the time of their deaths.

With that affirmation, John swings into the final points of his epistle. Now he wants to explore the confidence we can have in prayer.

> *Now this is the confidence that we have in Him, that if we ask anything according to His will, he hears us.*

John 5:14

What does it mean to have "*confidence*" in Him? What is praying "*according to His will?*" It sounds simple enough, but there is an enormous responsibility being placed upon believers, more than is upon the LORD. We've heard all our Christian lives that if we ask **anything** according to His will, it shall be granted to us. But what is the actual meaning of that condition? What do we have to do to be seeking something *according to His will*?

Look first at what it means to have "confidence" that such a prayer would be answered.

> *And when they had prayed, the place where they were assembled together was shaken; and they were all filled*

180

> *with the Holy Spirit, and they spoke the word of God*
> *with boldness.*

Acts 4:31

As the disciples gathered together after the Ascension of Christ in the Upper Room, they pray for guidance by God as to how they should proceed. The gift of the Holy Spirit was given to them and it gave them *"boldness."* Now, whether they prayed or whether they preached, they had a freedom in speaking, unreservedness in speech that allowed them to speak openly, frankly, i.e. without concealment, without ambiguity or circumlocution and without the use of figures and comparisons. The individual spirits were now filled with free and fearless confidence, cheerful courage, boldness, assurance. With that attitude now in them, they assumed the deportment by which one becomes conspicuous or secures publicity. This *boldness*, which we are to exercise in our prayers to the Almighty, not a human quality, is the result of being filled with the Holy Spirit. Should we exhibit that approach in our prayer life, because of our faith *and* our experience, we know God will answer our prayers.

> *And if we know that he hears us, whatever we ask, we*
> *know that we have the petitions that we have asked of*
> *Him.*

1ˢᵗ John 5:15

Our prayers are answered, or we consider them to be answered, because we know He has heard us, no matter what the prayer petition may be. We have the confidence to make these requests because we want only to please God, to bring glory to His name and for His purposes. The true purpose of prayer is *not* to force God to bring something to pass but for us to know more fully what pleases Him by offering our lives in service to Him. It is to be the opening of a channel of communication from Him to us, so what we do, how we do it, when and where we do it, will bring honor to Him, and further His purposes, not only for us, but for the coming of His kingdom.

To make his point clearer, John presents a specific example of the kind of intercessory prayer of which he speaks.

181

> *If anyone sees his brother sinning a sin which does not
> lead to death, he will ask, and he will give him life for
> those who commit sin not leading to death. There is sin
> leading to death. I do not say that he should pray about
> that.*

1ˢᵗ John 5:16

First, we need to understand the "*sin leading to death.*" John is
saying our concern for others ends when that sin is committed; our
prayers for their salvation and any service we perform in the name of
the Lord would be useless and pointless.

> *'Therefore I say to you, every sin and blasphemy will be
> forgiven men, but the blasphemy against the Spirit will
> not be forgiven men.*

Matthew 12:31

Matthew quotes Jesus who is identifying the sin which cannot be
forgiven. *Blasphemy* is used twice in the definition and it means
slander, detraction, speech injurious, to another's good name, impious
and reproachful speech injurious to divine majesty. In the first
instance, Christ says these kinds of verbal assaults can and will be set
aside at Judgment Day, but if one should make such an assault on the
character of God, then it shall not be cleansed. This is the
"Unforgivable Sin," blasphemy against the Holy Spirit. John in 1ˢᵗ
John 5:16 is saying there is no point to pray for forgiveness by those
who have done such; In the latter part of the verse, John is speaking of
other, "ordinary" sinfulness. The apostle appears to be making certain
this distinction is clear for two reasons. One, he hopes to discourage
those who curse God by denying the divinity of Jesus Christ. Secondly
he wants to reiterate the hopelessness of those who have done such
and discourage others who might want to follow in their erroneous
teachings.

Intercessory prayer was not a new concept to Christians. In the
Book of Job, the LORD instructs Eliphaz to seek it.

> *"Now therefore, take for yourselves seven bulls and
> seven rams, go to My servant Job, and offer up for*

182

yourselves a burnt offering; and My servant Job shall pray for you. For I will accept him, lest I deal with you according to your folly; because you have not spoken of Me what is right, as My servant Job has."

Job 42:8

Job is identified, by God no less, as one worthy of and a possessor of the power to plead a case before the LORD. He is cited as such because of his love for God and his fellow human beings.

'Therefore do not pray for this people, nor lift up a cry or prayer for them, nor make intercession to Me; for I will not hear you.

Jeremiah 7:16

Jeremiah, the Old Testament prophet, quotes the LORD's response to his intention to pray for relief of the suffering Hebrews. God declares His people to have consistently and purposefully rebelled and therefore are not worthy of redemption. Prayer for them *at this point in history* is futile and counterproductive. Judgment from the hand of God is sometimes necessary to bring about His purposes. It does not please Him to withhold His mercies, but His omniscience knows the ultimate result. Later, Jeremiah again records the word of the LORD:

Then the Lord said to me, "Do not pray for this people, for their good.

'When they fast, I will not hear their cry; and when they offer burnt offering and grain offering, I will not accept them. But I will consume them by the sword, by the famine, and by the pestilence.'

Then I said, "Ah, Lord God! Behold, the prophets say to them, "You shall not see the sword, nor shall you have famine, but I will give you assured peace in this place.'

And the Lord said to me, "The prophets prophesy lies in My name. I have not sent them, commanded them, nor spoken to them; they prophesy to you a false vision, divination, a worthless thing, and the deceit of their heart.

'Therefore thus says the Lord concerning the prophets who prophesy in My name, whom I did not send, and who say, "Sword and famine shall not be in this land'- 'By sword and famine those prophets shall be consumed!.

Jeremiah 14:11–15

The prophet and the LORD have a colloquy about Jeremiah's desire to pray for the people of Israel, in which God specifically states that he should not pray, for God's judgment is what is intended and best for them. Jeremiah questions why other prophets have spoken words that seem to be the opposite of his own message, and the LORD explains how these do not represent Him. In light of John's attempts to enlighten his contemporaries about false teachers, it is interesting this was a problem in the days of the Patriarchs as well.

All unrighteousness is sin, and there is sin not leading to death.

1ˢᵗ John 5:17

John presents to his readers the proposition that unrighteousness is sinfulness but concedes that not *every* sin will result in death. An *"unrighteous"* act is one a deed violating law and justice. It will bring about separation from God until confessed and repented of, but the performance of a sinful act does not automatically condemn one to eternal damnation. Even though failure to adhere to God's standards may lead one to a lifestyle that would deny them salvation, not every act is a sinful one punishable by death. From John's attitude revealed in this letter we know he personally considers those who teach falsely are deserving of death. Deliberate and intentional false teaching must involve the denial of the Holy Spirit because one has to turn their backs on the Spirit to preach doctrine contrary to God's Word. Denial and blaspheming the Holy Spirit is the "unpardonable sin" and those committing it deserve death. For them John has no sympathy, and offers no recourse.

> *We know that whoever is born of God does not sin; but he who has been born of God keeps himself, and the wicked one does not touch him.*
>
> *1ˢᵗ John 5:18*

John is winding down now, and as any good instructor, he begins to reiterate the key points of his lesson. Here he summarizes what we know about the characteristics of spiritual maturity. Those who belong to God's fellowship do not *intentionally* and *continually* sin. When we become one of God's children by accepting Christ as our Savior, we "keep" (attend to carefully, take care of, guard; keep one in the state in which he is in order to observe and behave appropriately) ourselves in that holy state. John's wording actually means we who are "begotten" or born of God (*born again!*) are defended and not touched by Satan.

We need to define "*whoever.*" Even though we have hinted at it by explaining the phrase "*born of God,*" its definition needs to be confirmed, and here Peter does so.

> *having been born again, not of corruptible seed but incorruptible, through the word of God which lives and abides forever,*
>
> *1ˢᵗ Peter 1:23*

A believer is one who has experienced rebirth through the reception, acknowledgment and devotion to the salvation granted by Jesus' sacrificial death. Peter reaffirms that the Word of God is just as eternal as its believers; he declares it to be alive and abiding (or existing) forever.

We also have to understand what John means by "*keeps.*" We believers seemingly need to do something specific to remain in this state. James sets the standard:

> *If anyone among you thinks he is religious, and does not bridle his tongue but deceives his own heart, this one's religion is useless.*

> *Pure and undefiled religion before God and the Father*
> *is this: to visit orphans and widows in their trouble, and*
> *to keep oneself unspotted from the world.*

> *James 1:26–27*

James tells us adhering to the standard of being a Christian demands control of our tongue (the words we speak). John has taught us this as well, that un-Christ like behavior cannot co-exist with behavior that expresses true love and compassion. Such hypocrisy weakens the fellowship and destroys a witness. James further notes that parts of our responsibilities include remaining estranged from the ways of the world that surround us. It is this disconnection that is so vital, for allowing society's influence into our lives only brings about a weakening of our Christian standards, making sinfulness attractive and easier to justify.

Our summarizing list of "what we know now" continues.

> *We know that we are of God, and the whole world lies*
> *under the sway of the wicked one.*

> *1ˢᵗ John 5:19*

Our relationship to God is confirmed. We are His and He is our LORD and Jesus is our Savior. But the rest of creation, that not belonging to the fellowship, the world, is manipulated by Satan and his standards. Does John literally mean Satan will control everything not committed to God?

> *'Now is the judgment of this world; now the ruler of*
> *this world will be cast out.*

> *John 12:31*

Jesus said it does. And Jesus proclaims Satan will be cast out of creation, and he is. John's *"Revelation of Jesus Christ"* details his vision of this forthcoming condemnation.

> *'I do not pray that You should take them out of the*
> *world, but that You should keep them from the evil one.*

> *'They are not of the world, just as I am not of the world.*

> *'Sanctify them by Your truth. Your word is truth.*
>
> *'As You sent Me into the world, I also have sent them into the world.*
>
> *'And for their sakes I sanctify Myself, that they also may be sanctified by the truth.*
>
> *John 17:15–20*

In His High Priestly Prayer, Jesus reveals there is as much danger in satanic influence as there is in actual satanic presence. His prayer was that we, believers, the little children of the faith, be protected against the enticements of the darkness. We cannot be removed from the world (until the time of our death or Christ's return, whichever comes first) so we must live in it but not succumb to its allure.

Satan is the ruler of the world. No one can deny the sphere of evil that pervades our society, and it comes from his design. Because of the Fall, there is only one alternative for those not surrendering to Jesus, and that is experiencing the ultimate judgment of God.

> *'Now is the judgment of this world; now the ruler of this world will be cast out.*
>
> *John 12:31*

Jesus explained to His disciples what the state of the world would be during the period from His Ascension until His return:

> *'I will no longer talk much with you, for the ruler of this world is coming, and he has nothing in Me.*
>
> *'But that the world may know that I love the Father, and as the Father gave Me commandment, so I do. Arise, let us go from here.*
>
> *John 14:30–31*

"The rule of the world," Satan, was coming to take over dominion of it, to try to wrest it from God's hand by making his blackness so attractive and appealing that people would prefer it to the opportunity for eternal life with God in heaven. Until the time of their final battle, Jesus will have no communication, no exchange or interaction with

Satan directly. His war will be waged through us, the believers, and the Holy Spirit dwelling in us. Jesus, knowing what lay before Him at this moment, nevertheless told His followers He was prepared to accept it because it would testify as to His love for the Father, and the Father's love for His creation. Salvation was just ahead, even though it seemed the power of Satan was in control.

So we must endure today, burdened and weighted down with the knowledge that so much is wrong and God's standards are being trampled upon. Yet out hearts must express themselves in the same way the black preacher did as he proclaimed one Good Friday in his church's services,

> 'Today is Friday. The Savior of the World is dead. He has been taken down from the cross and laid in a borrowed grave. All the world is plunged into darkness. It would seem all is lost.
>
> "**BUT** Sunday's coming! Sunday is coming!"

John keeps on recapitulating our lessons.

> *And we know that the Son of God has come and has given us an understanding, that we may know Him who is true; and we are in Him who is true, in His Son Jesus Christ. This is the true God and eternal life.*
>
> *1ˢᵗ John 5:20*

Through the presence and revelation of the Holy Spirit we know who Jesus Christ was, that He was the Son of God, fully divine and fully human. We know that He has come to Earth and through His teaching and His gift of the Holy Spirit He has given us understanding and comprehension of difficult spiritual concepts.

> *And He opened their understanding, that they might comprehend the Scriptures.*
>
> *Luke 24:45*

As Jesus taught His disciples after His resurrection, they were able to see for the first time the true meaning of passages they had read all their lives in the Old Testament; enlightenment came to them. It was only through the application of the power of the Holy Spirit on Pentecost that they then received the power to apply these interpretations in ways to spread the Gospel throughout the world.

> *'And you shall love the Lord your God with all your heart, with all your soul, with all your mind, and with all your strength." This is the first commandment.*
>
> **Mark 12:30**

For centuries men and women have repeated this commandment (and in Mark's Gospel Jesus is again reciting it for His disciples). But there must be an understanding of what is meant by *"your mind."* In this case it is the Greek word meaning the mind as a faculty of understanding, feeling, desiring; understanding; mind, i.e. spirit, way of thinking and feeling; and thoughts, either good or bad. When *"activated"* by the Holy Spirit, our entire mind-set changes from the negative aspect of carnality to the positive focus of divine character.

John tells us that we know "He who is true."

> *'And this is eternal life, that they may know You, the only true God, and Jesus Christ whom You have sent.*
>
> **John 17:3**

This is getting cyclical again but John wants us to understand that God sent His Son, who actually *is* God. If God is truth and cannot lie, then that which is of Him must also be true (or truth), so Jesus Christ is the embodiment of truth.

Put together the fact that we know who Jesus is, and that we know we have "understanding.'

> *'And to the angel of the church in Philadelphia write, "These things says He who is holy, He who is true, "He who has the key of David, He who opens and no one shuts, and shuts and no one opens':*
>
> **Revelation 3:7**

189

The letter Christ dictates to John in his Revelation to the church at Philadelphia opens with the statement of the power one has in knowing the truth. It enables one to discern and grasp and make dear to them those things which they should embrace, and permits them to put aside, and not be attracted to, those which are not worthy.

The phrase the One "who is holy" goes back to the very familiar Book of Psalms.

> *For You will not leave my soul in Sheol, Nor will You allow Your Holy One to see corruption.*

> **Psalms 16:10**

This is one of the first references in the Old Testament (perhaps not chronologically but in the physical arrangement of the scriptures) to the prophecy that He who is of God would not rot in the grave but would be resurrected. Only one man has ever been able to avoid that, and that was Jesus Christ. The writer of the letter to the Philadelphians needed to be identified clearly; it was The Holy One.

> *Of the increase of His government and peace There will be no end, Upon the throne of David and over His kingdom, To order it and establish it with judgment and justice From that time forward, even forever. The zeal of the Lord of hosts will perform this.*

> **Isaiah 9:7**

This passage from the Old Testament prophecy of Isaiah speaks of the Messiah plainly. Here, in the translation being used for this book, the Bible identifies that He shall represent the "throne of David" in Isaiah and "the key of David" in Revelation. Both mean the same; that individual shall have the authority, power, and control of the King of Israel, a chain going all the way back to David. David was selected by God to be King of Israel, and, despite his human failings, God still declared David to be "a man after my own heart.'

The key of the house of David I will lay on his shoulder;
So he shall open, and no one shall shut; And he shall
shut, and no one shall open.

Isaiah 22:22

Isaiah further identifies this person who shall be crowned king. In the scheme of Old Testament prophecy, often the time interval between events was hidden, similar to the view one has of a mountain range. Individual crests are discernible but there is no clue as to the distance or space between them. Additionally, heavenly prophecies sometimes were fulfilled many times. In this passage Isaiah is faced with both issues. The message from God refers to both an earthly king *and* a Heavenly King, both of whom will meet the criteria.

God's omnipotence is also to be considered.

Behold, he breaketh down, and it cannot be built again:
he shutteth up a man, and there can be no opening.

Job 12:14

Job, the Old Testament sufferer, made many correct statements about the nature of God. Even though he was frustrated and then challenges God's decision for his life, Job admits that the LORD is the ultimate builder and the ultimate destroyer. What he creates is created; what he eliminates is gone forever.

All these things we know now, John says. They all confirm Christ is who He says He is. He is the source, *the only source*, of eternal life. His pattern and instructions show us how to live a spiritual life. The way Jesus leads is the only way to heaven and to ever-lasting fellowship with the Almighty.

Little children, keep yourselves from idols. Amen.

1ˢᵗ John 5:21

John closes his letter with a final plea. Anything worshiped or highly regarded that is *not* of God's revealed will is an idol. From the very beginning of His relationship with the Hebrews, God warned against falling into the trap of placing anything ahead of their loyalty and devotion to Him. The nation of Israel suffered much because it failed to understand this danger and descended into idol worship. John, the caring patriarch of Christianity, using again his precious term of affection, implores his little children to not engage in worshiping anything other than God and Christ. And in those trying days of persecution of which John doubtless was aware, the temptation would be strong for Christians, offered the choice of death or recanting their faith to make the wrong decision.

With a final sighing *"amen,"* John lays down his stylus, folds his hands, closes his eyes and asks the LORD to bless his work. A trusted aide lifts it gently from his lap. The process of copying it begins, and soon John's love letter to believers everywhere is on its way to history, and ultimately, to our ears and eyes.

A Letter of Love

We sit back, close our Bibles, and reflect on what John has taught us in his first epistle. It is a masterfully simple document, refreshing us on the basic elements of Christianity's essential tenets. Its points are driven home with repetition, almost to a maddening point, yet we realize how central they are to our faith and how critical it is for us to grasp and then defend them. Reviewing it should rekindle our baby Christian enthusiasm. There should be in our spirit a renewal of that initial excitement we had when we first grasped the significance of what it means to be a Christian.

John was the last surviving disciple. he'd outlived all the other major players in the drama of Christ's ministry. It is almost as if Jesus' statement in John 21:22 (*"If I will that he remain till I come, what is that to you? You follow Me."*) was coming true. I don't know but what it was a grace from the LORD for John to live as long as he did, to give him the joy of seeing the little band of believers grow to the swelling congregations all across the Mediterranean. Doubtless even Mary the mother of Jesus had died before he began his traveling ministry; he would not have abandoned her after Jesus had put her care into his hands. His care for her (mysteriously but characteristically) has never been recorded authentically. Judging from his insistent emphasis on love and service to others, what he did for her most certainly was beyond anyone expectations. Perhaps his long life was a "thank you" from Jesus.

Another note of God's special affection for this man was that he, according to most accounts, was the only original apostle who died a natural death after he had the opportunity to teach a second generation of leaders. What better training could men like Polycarp have had but the direct testimony and witness of John to them?

One looks back on this book and wonders, again, *"Why did John write this?"* The obvious reasons are he sought to counteract the influence of the Gnostics, to re-affirm the dual nature of Christ as fully God and fully man, to clarify principles of godly living, and to warn of the danger of false teachers. Each is a worthwhile goal; each is accomplished in the five chapters. Each one, by itself, would have been a worthy topic.

But I feel there may be even another motivation. John, by his own appellation, was the disciple of love. He loved Jesus in a way seemingly deeper and more profound than the other eleven. But that doesn't mean they didn't care for him. John just seemed to be more in alignment with Christ's affections. As he aged, his sensitivity likely grew and his true love for his "little children" increased. His phrase, *"little children,"* used so often in this first letter, is more than a term used to identify the spiritual age of a segment of his audience. It was a term of kindly, affectionate address by teachers to their disciples, sprinkled with sincere warmth.

In my own mind I picture John as being a large man. After all, he was a commercial fisherman, so he was no physical wimp. He was in good physical shape. Remember he outran Peter to the Tomb on Resurrection morning. At this point in his life he would have long, flowing white hair and beard. His eyes would be dark under heavy white eyebrows. His size would have been a contradiction of his nature. He would be physically intimidating but once he opened his mouth and spread his arms wide to offer an embrace, it would be obvious this is a man of love.

To support my contention, examine the crucifixion scene. John was the only disciple to be present; the others had fled into hiding, fearing for their own lives. Why didn't John? He states over and over in his gospel of how much he loved Jesus, how they seemed to have a special bond. He wanted to be there. Because his physical size would have intimidated the vermin-like religious leaders in flowing ephods and towering headgear, even Roman soldiers likely gave him a wide berth as he approached the site with Jesus' mother. While the others ran and hid, he accompanied Mary as her shield and protector. Roman centurions were not all blood thirty animals; they had mothers and daughters, too. As this giant of a man waded into the crowd, the people parted and let him pass. He likely spoke not a word to anyone but his presence spoke volumes of who he was and why he was there.

Jesus recognized His mother and spoke to her, directing her attention to John, then gave His command of care to His disciple. John's appearance must have been distinctive enough for Christ to have spotted him in the crowd, through His pain dulled vision and the growing gloom.

John was courageous, being there at the cross. Surely he knew the danger of being classified as a follower. Yet he was there. And he didn't shrink for the responsibility of caring for His Master's mother even though this likely put him in daily conflict with the ruling religious leaders. As a widow (even with other children who were now likely grown) Mary would have been entitled to assistance from the temple's priests. Who she was offered the Levites reason enough to deny her the small amount of money, meat and grain to which she was entitled. In my imagination I can visualize her approaching for the first distribution after all the Passover passion. Slowly, quietly, almost timidly, she would keep her place in line. When her turn came, she stood not alone but by her side was a mountain of man, dark piercing eyes. They knew who he was as well as who she was. No words needed to be spoken, no reminders of what was the Law. But John remained silent. He made no threats, no demands. And the Pharisees and Sadducees made no move to arrest him. *They knew, they knew.* Mary got her portion and John walked away with her. And so it would go, each time of distribution. John did what he did because he loved Jesus and he loved Mary, and he loved others.

For us today, what is so hard to grasp is the simplicity of John's message, of his *life*. We can satisfy all the requirements of the Old Testament Law and be in full compliance with the New Covenant as well if we only loved one another. This is love more than Rodney King's "Can't we all just get along?" This is the love that puts aside our own priorities, that has no ulterior motive. This is the love that forgives even before the offense is given. This is the love marriage partners should have for one another, forgiving anything, forgiving everything.

Many have said of a great hurt done against them, "I can forgive but I can never forget." Saying that means one is willing to move forward, but the hurt will always be there. The only reason we should "never forget" a recollection of painful experiences should be a way of protecting ourselves from being deceived or hurt again. But to cling to such things as a way of punishing ourselves and the offender is not forgiveness. That is not love. To truly love, to truly forgive, one must never even be able to recall the offense. God tells us when we accept His Son as our Savior <u>all</u> our sins are as far from His memory as the East is from the West. That's love.

This is what John really wanted to teach in his writings. The world's evils could be overcome by replacing all the conflicts with love, forgiveness, dispensation to the ultimate degree. If a society could put aside the frictions existing within its layers, it could become totally productive. Harmony would be not just a goal but an eve-present condition.

This is what John sought. Not only to bring back into the fold those believers who were enticed away from the basics by thrilling new (but dangerously flawed) teachers and doctrine, but to encourage love and affection among all. He will write two more letters to his little children, each one as filled with emotion and affection as 1st John. Each is just as rich with teaching, guidance, warning and reassurance. But 1st John is the primer for Christians who may feel a bit estranged from their beliefs, tossed about by the seemingly contradictory teachings coming from all corners. It is the one new believers need to study immediately after consuming John's gospel.

It is the love letter written on each of our hearts.

About The Author

B ill Andrew was born in Atlanta, Georgia in 1947. His earliest ambition was to be a radio announcer and he spent a considerable portion of his teen-aged years pursuing that goal, finally attending the University of Georgia and receiving an MA degree in Journalism, with a specialty in Broadcasting. His minors were American history and political science. His goal was to be a political reporter and commentator.

A career in radio did not last long.

He married, and went to work with his father in the motion picture theater business, representing small "mom and pop" theaters in Georgia, Alabama, and Tennessee. In 1972 he found work as the manager of the recorded products division of a publishing house dedicated to motivational and inspirational topics. After a short time there he returned to the family business only to leave in 1978 for the publishing house of the Presbyterian Church, U.S., then headquartered in Atlanta. Bill was the Advertising and Direct Mail Manager, writing promotional copy for the new books as they were published.

Reunification of the divided Presbyterians meant relocation of the denomination's headquarters to Louisville, Kentucky, so Bill found work as Public Relations and Information Program Coordinator for an agency of Georgia's state government. Budgets being what they are, administrative decisions were made to eliminate public relations for the division, so Bill moved out as a freelance public relations consultant.

Freelancing wasn't really working so Bill stepped into commercial insurance as a property and casualty broker, working with several agencies but his real love was writing. He retired as a marketing coordinator from an insurance agency in 2008. His exposure to biblical studies at the Presbyterian's publishing house inspired him to begin his pursuit of writing and studying in more depth.

Bill lives in Roswell, Georgia, with his wife of 41 years Sandy. They have been members in the past of Peachtree Road United Methodist

Church (Atlanta), Coldwater United Methodist Church (Elberton, Georgia), Sentell Baptist Church (Atlanta), Mount Paran Church of God (Atlanta). They have attended services at Atlanta Street Baptist Church (Roswell), North Point Community Church (Alpharetta) and First Baptist Church (Atlanta). Their son and daughter-in-law have one daughter and one son.

End Notes

[1]   *Spirit Filled Life Bible: New King James Version*, Thomas Nelson Publishers (Nashville), 1992.

[2]   *Understanding and Applying the Bible: An Introduction to Hermeneutics,* J. Robertson McQuilkin, Moody Press (Chicago), 1983.

[3]   *The Discovery Bible: New Testament*, Gary Hill, Moody Press (Chicago), 1987.

[4]   Unless otherwise noted, all scripture quotations are from the (Modern) New King James Version. Citations will be identified as NKJV.

[5]   *The People's New Testament Commentary,* M. Boring & Fred Craddock, Westminster John Knox Press (Louisville), 2004.

[6]   *The New Strong's Exhaustive Concordance of the Bible*, James Strong, LL.D., S.T.D, Thomas Nelson Publishers (Nashville), 1995.

[7]   *Ibid.*

[8]   John 13:34; Romans 13:8; 1st Thessalonians 4:9; 1st Peter 1:22.

[9]   The writer of Hebrews makes the same complaint of his audience. And Paul sometimes chastises his flocks for not being as spiritually mature as they should.

[10]   The similarity between this passage and Hebrews 11 leads me to personally believe Paul is the author of Hebrews. Both single out Abraham and recount how he accepted as true that which he could never perceive – a future of generations springing from him that would be innumerable. In actual fact, the author remains "unknown.' Whoever wrote the book knew Hebraic tradition and scripture. They cemented it together to the essentials of Christianity and it, like 1st John, is an excellent handbook of basic Christian principles.

[11]   Most writers refer to the Holy Spirit with a masculine pronoun form, which is quite proper and correct. Personally, I find this a bit confusing and somehow irreverent. Though I am no champion of the current trend to "political correctness,' I prefer and use a gender neutral third person.

[12]   It has also proven to be a strong means of teaching congregations. Through these recitations, others learn of the power of God's forgiveness; the "illustrations" are not part of the sermon, but living, breathing accounts of the transforming power of accepting Jesus Christ as Lord and Savior.

[13]   *The New Strong's Exhaustive Concordance of the Bible*, James Strong, LL.D., S.T.D, Thomas Nelson Publishers (Nashville), 1995.

[14]   *Ibid.*

[15]   *The New Scofield*[R] *Study Bible: King James Version*, Oxford University Press (New York), 1967.

[16]   Many teachers now refer to this prayer as "The Lord's Prayer," identifying the more familiar passage in Matthew 6 and Luke 11 as "The Model Prayer."

---

[17] Because of His holy nature, God could not communicate with the sinful being Christ had become as He died for our sins. So, while on the Cross, God turned His back to Jesus. The Holy Spirit did not depart, only the communion with God ceased for a time. But Jesus, fully human as well as fully divine, experienced the agony of physical ***and*** spiritual separation from His Father.

[18] Though they were cousins, and likely had met long before either began their ministries, the revelation of Who Jesus truly was may not have been given to John until the time of Christ's baptism. It would have been unlikely Mary and Elizabeth would have shared their divine intelligences with their families to such an extent. Their fathers certainly knew the truth, but at the time of the events recorded in the gospel, we have no evidence the Baptist's parents were alive, and only Mary the Mother of Jesus seems to be alive. The two boys obviously knew of their calling early on in their lives.

CPSIA information can be obtained at www.ICGtesting.com
Printed in the USA
LVOW070910081212

310698LV00002B/73/P